FOUR CUPS

CHRIS HODGES

New York Times bestselling author

FOUR CUPS

God's Timeless Promises for a Life of Fulfillment

TYNDALE
MOMENTUM

An Imprint of
Tyndale House Publishers, Inc.

Visit Tyndale online at www.tyndale.com.

Visit Tyndale Momentum online at www.tyndalemomentum.com.

TYNDALE is a registered trademark of Tyndale House Publishers, Inc. *Tyndale Momentum* and the Tyndale Momentum logo are trademarks of Tyndale House Publishers, Inc. Tyndale Momentum is an imprint of Tyndale House Publishers, Inc.

Four Cups: God's Timeless Promises for a Life of Fulfillment

Designed by Nicole Grimes

Published in association with the literary agency of Winters and King, Inc., 2448 E. 81st St., Suite 5900, Tulsa, OK 74137.

Library of Congress Cataloging-in-Publication Data

Hodges, Chris.
  Four cups : God's timeless promises for a life of fulfillment / Chris Hodges.
    pages cm
  Includes bibliographical references.
  ISBN 978-1-4143-7127-6 (sc)
  1. God (Christianity)—Promises. I. Title.
  BT180.P7H63 2014
  231.7—dc23   2013042507

Printed in the United States of America

20	19	18	17	16	15	14
9	8	7	6			

To the pastors and team at Church of the Highlands:
You share my vision and heart for these principles.
Your love for God and people is changing the world.
I am honored to do life and ministry with you.

CONTENTS

FOREWORD

I will lift up the cup of salvation and call on the name of the Lord.

PSALM 116:13, ESV

I HAVE BECOME FASCINATED recently with the "table of the Lord." God's covenant usually comes down to a meal, a "cup" that seals and guarantees all of His covenant promises. This cup was the guarantee of the "new covenant" that Jesus served His disciples: "This cup is the new covenant in my blood" (Luke 22:20, NIV).

The book you are holding is one of the best explanations of God's covenant "cup" you will ever read. This powerful cup is rich with meaning, all made clear in the first Passover meal that Israel had in Egypt.

Having pastored for more than thirty years, I have seen people struggle with each of these four areas: freedom from sin, deliverance from bondage, finding their purpose, and living a life of fulfillment. The "cup of the Lord" is actually four separate cups, each of which promises freedom, deliverance, purpose, and fulfillment! *Wow!*

I am convinced that if each believer, each church in the world, could grasp these four powerful principles, the church would move into nothing short of revival. I have seen average, moderate, lukewarm, half-interested believers turn into powerful, passionate, and proactive believers when they became convinced of their *total* freedom from their past, were *delivered* from their bondage, *discovered* their life's purpose, and *launched* into a life of service!

Since 2001, Church of the Highlands has grown from a handful of believers on a "launch team" to tens of thousands in weekly attendance, through these four principles. They are not complicated; they are life-changing. Having ministered at Highlands numerous times, I've seen some of the most passionate, powerful, and proactive members you will find anywhere in the world.

I have known pastor Chris Hodges since he was saved at Bethany at fifteen years of age. He served faithfully as our youth pastor, and as one of our most effective associate pastors. His life, marriage, ministry, and motives are impeccable. His wife, Tammy, his mother (his father is now in heaven), his siblings, and children are all deeply involved in the Highlands dynamo that is reaching the entire state of Alabama—and now America and the world.

Don't put this book down until you drink from all four cups! God's plan for your life, your future destiny, your joyful fulfillment, and your eternal reward could all depend on how slowly and carefully you digest this book. If God spread a table in front of you and offered you these four cups, wouldn't you drink every drop?

It's not an accident that this book made its way into your

hands. I believe that Jesus Christ, who shed His precious covenant blood for you, is saying right now, "Give me a little time with you. Have a meal with me. Receive all of my promises and blessings. Let me change your life, change your past, and enlighten your future."

Pull up a chair.

Larry Stockstill

CHAPTER ONE

PROMISES,
PROMISES

I praise your name for your unfailing love

and faithfulness; for your promises are

backed by all the honor of your name.

PSALM 138:2

GOD HAS MADE YOU SOME PROMISES. He made them at the very beginning—not the beginning of your life, but from the beginning of faith itself. They are promises that are close to his heart, and they have never changed. They are the key to your fulfillment in life—both this life and in the life to come.

God promises to rescue you from bondage.

He promises to deliver you from whatever holds you back.

He promises to help you discover his original intention for your life.

And he promises to make you part of a family that is making a difference in the world.

God's promises are at the center of what we often call "the mystery of faith," the way we live our lives in response to God's loving pursuit of us. Though God spoke his promises to his people thousands of years ago, generation after generation, according to the apostle Paul, missed their significance.

The wisdom we speak of is the mystery of God— his plan that was previously hidden, even though he made it for our ultimate glory before the world began. But the rulers of this world have not understood it; if they had, they would not have crucified our glorious Lord. That is what the Scriptures mean when they say,

> *"No eye has seen, no ear has heard,*
>   *and no mind has imagined*
> *what God has prepared*
>   *for those who love him."*

I CORINTHIANS 2:7-9

✳ ✳ ✳

Maybe you're thinking that promises don't mean much anymore.

Every day, men and women promise to stay together for the rest of their lives, and yet many couples fall apart after only a few years. Political leaders promise hope and change, to reverse the slippery slope of economic decline and restore the public's trust, and yet most rarely follow through on their campaign promises—at least not until the next election rolls around. Businesses promise to take care of their employees, and everyone talks about creating new jobs, but downsizing and outsourcing have become the norm.

Chances are you've heard plenty of promises in the past. And chances are that some, if not all, of those promises have been broken. At home, at work, even in the church, people have a tough time keeping their promises.

If we define a promise as "an offer with a guaranteed result," it's not surprising that God is the only one who always keeps his promises. When he makes a promise, he always fulfills it. It may not be fulfilled in the way we want or expect, or on the timetable we'd choose, but God always comes through. When he gives you his word, he keeps it.

> *God is not a man, so he does not lie. He is not human,*
> *so he does not change his mind. Has he ever spoken*
> *and failed to act? Has he ever promised and not*
> *carried it through?*
>
> NUMBERS 23:19

✳ ✳ ✳

When someone makes a promise, it piques our interest. For example, when someone says, "I promise you'll like it," we know he or she wants to intrigue us, stimulate our imagination, and get us to try something new. When God makes promises, he hopes to pique our interest so that we'll experience the fullness of the exciting journey he's designed for us.

We're all on a spiritual journey. And no matter where *you* are along the way—whether you've been a follower of Jesus for most of your life or you've just recently surrendered to him, or maybe you're somewhere in between— you're probably longing for more. Maybe you're in survival mode: You're just trying to keep your head above water by holding down a job, paying the bills, and providing for the kids. Or maybe you're in a spiritual rut: Your faith used to be vibrant, but now feels kind of stale. Maybe you're experiencing wonderful joy on your journey with God, but wish you knew how to share your faith more effectively with others.

Regardless of where you are, you're not alone in wanting to move forward. We all want to know where we are, where we're going, and how we're going to get there. We want to be empowered for life's journey and equipped by God to do more than just survive. We want to experience the abundant joy, peace, and satisfaction he promised us.

Though it's tempting to think that the process of spiritual development involves obeying a bunch of rules and guidelines, it's much simpler than that. When we read the history of God's chosen people, the nation of Israel, in the Bible, we discover that God made four significant promises to his children.

At the time, the Israelites were enslaved in Egypt. Many years before, they had migrated south from Canaan in order to survive a terrible famine that had devastated the land. As the Hebrew population increased, however, the Egyptians felt threatened and eventually forced the Jewish people to become slaves. But God was not about to leave his chosen people in bondage in a foreign land.

God raised up Moses to lead the people of Israel to a new home, a promised land. After a protracted negotiation with Pharaoh in which God revealed his power by unleashing a series of plagues on the Egyptians, Moses came to a stalemate with the stubborn leader who still refused to free the Israelites. As a final inducement, the Angel of Death was allowed to visit each household, Egyptian and Hebrew alike, and claim the life of every firstborn male. However, the angel was instructed to "pass over" any home where the doorpost had been painted with the blood of a lamb, thereby allowing those children to live. At the time of this dreadful display of his power, God made it clear that not only would he spare his people, but he would also lead them to a life of freedom they could not even imagine.

So God made them four promises:

1. "I will free you from your oppression."
2. "I will rescue you from your slavery in Egypt."
3. "I will redeem you with a powerful arm and great acts of judgment."
4. "I will claim you as my own people, and I will be your God."

These four "I will" statements in Exodus 6:6-7 laid the foundation for the nation of Israel and became crucial elements of their annual celebration of God's faithfulness—which they still observe today—known as Passover. At this yearly event four cups of wine are used to commemorate and celebrate God's four promises. These four cups of promise, as they're called, bridge ancient history with the yet-to-come future. For Jewish families, it's like celebrating Independence Day, a time to remember when God brought them out of slavery and into freedom, redemption, and fulfillment.

These four cups hold the same promise for those of us today who have surrendered our lives to God and been grafted into his family through the death, burial, and resurrection of Jesus Christ. By placing our faith in Jesus, we have become recipients of these "offers with a guaranteed result," which begin with God's declaration of what he will do for us if we will let him. These promises are foundational to God's desire to know and love his children. Though most Christians aren't familiar with them, the details of the Passover celebration hold the key to what God wants to do in our lives right now.

✻ ✻ ✻

Each of the four cups reveals God's presence in a distinct and dramatic way. As we discover more of the historical background and biblical significance behind the four cups, I want to show you how each cup is also uniquely *personal*. It's not only fascinating as background, but I'm convinced these four promises also reveal the process of interactive development—spiritual transformation—that continues to take place between God and us.

Though we're all on a spiritual journey, no one has arrived at perfection yet—nor will we in this lifetime. As Paul writes, "I press on to possess that perfection for which Christ Jesus first possessed me. No, dear brothers and sisters, I have not achieved it, but I focus on this one thing: Forgetting the past and looking forward to what lies ahead, I press on to reach the end of the race and receive the heavenly prize for which God, through Christ Jesus, is calling us"

> *By placing our faith in Jesus, we have become recipients of these "offers with a guaranteed result."*

(Philippians 3:12-14). God calls each of us to grow and mature in our relationship with him. No matter where we may be on our spiritual journey, the four cups of promise provide a simple, powerful, unforgettable way of tracking our progress in growing closer to God.

Whenever I'm asked about the meaning behind the name of our church, Church of the Highlands, I'm reminded of my passion for helping others grow. I started the church with other like-minded believers because we wanted to reach new heights and take people to higher ground. Our church is rooted in the common desire that says, "There has to be more."

Are you satisfied with where you are? Or would you like to reach higher ground?

* * *

From my experience, our spiritual journey is like mountain climbing. When I lived in Colorado, I loved scaling some of the "fourteeners," the more than fifty Rocky Mountain peaks above 14,000 feet of elevation. Although I climbed only eight of them, I've never worked harder or been more exhilarated. Well above the tree line, the narrow footholds became sharper (making each step more treacherous) and the air became thinner (making it harder and harder to breathe) the higher I climbed. But the unbelievably stunning beauty at the summit? Wow! There's nothing like the view from the top—jagged, snowcapped peaks in shades of purple, blue, and gray, stretching out as far as the eye can see. As difficult as each climb was, after I came back down, I couldn't wait for the next one.

I want to take you on a journey to the summit of some spiritual fourteeners. Each step along the way will be both challenging and rewarding. But as you learn to walk in the promises of God, you won't believe how beautiful the view can be.

God wants so much more for us than we realize. We often get hung up on our circumstances and live with blinders on to the big picture. As we climb and explore and learn to drink from the four cups of promise, my hope is that your thirst will be quenched and you will experience a wellspring of joy, peace, and hope in the midst of the purposeful life you were created to live.

The Christian life was never intended to be a flat, rutted path of obligation, disappointment, and mediocrity. Don't settle for less than God's best for you. Don't stifle that voice in your heart that tells you there has to be more. Don't stay on the treadmill of conformity, trudging along to someone else's idea of who you should be. God wants your relationship with him to be every bit as adventurous and exhilarating as climbing Mount Everest. The journey won't be easy, but it promises to be life-changing.

The Israelites probably expected Moses to lead them to

> *Don't settle for less than God's best for you. Don't stifle that voice in your heart that tells you there has to be more.*

their new home in Canaan right away. But as you might recall, it wasn't that simple. It took forty years of trailblazing in the desert, and then a faith-based fight, before they were able to claim the Promised Land. And along the way the children of Israel grumbled and stumbled and second-guessed God most of the time.

I suspect they thought much like we do. In the Bible, God makes his promises seem so simple. So simple, in fact, that we tend to expect *immediate* fulfillment. When that doesn't happen, we may begin to hear God's promises as purely rhetorical—or merely historical. In any case, they become one more sound bite in the weekly mix of information overload.

But God's promises are real. When life doesn't make sense, we must hold on to those promises as the basis of our faith in God and our hope for what he is going to do.

But God's promises are real. And when life doesn't make sense, we must hold on to those promises as the basis of our faith in God and our hope for what he is going to do. The Hebrew people grew up hearing and telling the stories of God's promises to Abraham. But somewhere during those four hundred years of slavery in Egypt, the stories must have become little more than fables of a more illustrious past.

When God doesn't act on our timetable, it's tempting to dismiss his promises as untrue or irrelevant. But that's what our enemy, the devil, wants us to believe! Instead, like

Abraham, we must keep the promises of God before us, *especially* during trials. "Abraham never wavered in believing God's promise. In fact, his faith grew stronger, and in this he brought glory to God. He was fully convinced that God is able to do whatever he promises" (Romans 4:20-21).

Our faith is not simply a *mental agreement* with a set of facts. It is a firm reliance and trust in a *person*—namely, God—and his ability to do what he says he will do. Faith is *leaning* and *depending* on God and his promises. If you're ready to join me on this journey to discover more about the reality of God's faithfulness, let's start by looking at how, when, where, and why God made these four promises to us—and what each one means for reaching our personal summit with him.

To help you get started, here's a prayer you can use as a model for asking God to reveal his promises to you:

Father, you know where I am and all that's going on in my life—the big things, the little things, the secrets, and the burdens. I trust you to meet me right where I am and reveal your promises to me. I don't want to settle for less than your best, Lord, so guide my steps and lead me to your higher ground. Amen.

CHAPTER TWO

FINALLY FREE

The Israelites continued to groan under their

burden of slavery. They cried out for help,

and their cry rose up to God. God heard

their groaning, and he remembered his

covenant promise to Abraham, Isaac,

and Jacob. He looked down on the people

of Israel and knew it was time to act.

EXODUS 2:23-25

JUST ABOUT EVERY PERSON, Christian or not, is familiar with the story of Moses leading the children of Israel out of Egypt. We all remember the Sunday school images or scenes from the movie *The Ten Commandments,* but have you ever wondered what it was really like? I imagine it was something like this . . .

> The noonday sun scorched the dry riverbeds and beat down on the backs of the Hebrew slaves. Sunlight shimmered with blinding intensity on the mounds of sand and clay being molded into bricks. The desiccated hulls of dead frogs and insects blanketed the ground, and the stench was unbearable. The Egyptian overseer scratched at ugly boils festering on his arms and neck. A stand of palm trees provided scant shade for the dozens of men working the bricks, and there was no breeze to provide relief from the desert sun.
>
> One of the slaves, Josiah, knew there would not be many more days like this one. Through the grapevine he had heard of a man named Moses—one of their own, though reared in the Egyptian palace—who had the hand of the Lord upon him. Moses had spoken to Pharaoh and demanded that he release the Hebrew people to return to their homeland. When the monarch had laughed at such a request and threatened to have Moses imprisoned and tortured, Moses' staff

had suddenly twisted and come alive in his hand, transforming instantly into a mighty serpent that writhed toward Pharaoh.

Both men had come away from the encounter unharmed, but Moses made it clear that there would be much deadlier consequences than the venom of a snake if Pharaoh did not heed the Lord's command to free the Israelites. Then the plagues had started. The river and all waters turned to blood. The sky rained with frogs and insects and rumbled with thunder that shook buildings to their foundations.

Pharaoh went back and forth, one minute agreeing to free the Hebrew slaves and then rescinding his decision as soon as the latest plague ended. But now word had spread that the worst and most deadly plague was yet to come. Because Pharaoh had not heeded God's command, death would soon visit every household in Egypt, claiming the firstborn child within each home. However, Yahweh had provided a way for his people to save their children: If they painted their doorposts with the blood of a sacrificial lamb, the death angel would pass them by.

Sweat trickled down Josiah's tan, muscled back. His shoulders ached from lifting bricks and stacking them on pallets to be carried to the new building sites in Pithon. His people had endured the indignity of slavery long enough. The Egyptians treated their animals better than they treated the Hebrews. And Josiah's brother had been beaten to death for allegedly disrespecting his master.

But their God had not forgotten them. He had promised to save them, to preserve his people, to lead them to freedom and a land flowing with milk and honey. The time was coming. The day was half over and soon the sun would set and darkness would descend. The Lord was going to make good his promise to free them and lead them to a place where they could live in harmony and peace with one another. God's promise was about to be fulfilled that very night.

* * *

Maybe it was nothing like that, but it's hard not to wonder what the people of Israel were thinking and feeling when God finally activated his promises to them. Surely there were times when they wanted to despair. They probably tried to remember God's goodness from the past, but it must have been tough with whip-bearing Egyptian masters surrounding them. Yes, they knew the stories of how God had saved their ancestors from a terrible famine that had ravaged their homeland, and how one of their own, Joseph, had been put in charge of all of Egypt's grain. It had indeed been a gift that their people were able to migrate to this foreign land in order to survive.

At first, things had been good for the descendants of Jacob (Israel) in the land of Egypt. There had been abundant food, and thanks to the influence of Joseph, the pharaoh had been kindly disposed toward the Hebrew people, who found plenty of land to settle along the Nile River. But now, almost four hundred years later, the people had spent far more generations as slaves in Egypt than they had ever enjoyed as free people. As the generations passed, and a succession of pharaohs took the throne, they imposed harsh measures against the Hebrews, who could either serve their new Egyptian masters or be killed.

Surely the Lord had not saved them from starvation and led them to this land only to have them die as slaves.

Surely the Lord had not saved them from starvation and led them to this land only to have them die as slaves. But as the years turned into decades, and the decades into centuries, it became increasingly difficult to maintain hope. The more their numbers grew, the tighter Pharaoh's grip became.

But then, just as he had promised, God raised a leader from among them. Despite Moses' initial objections, he was uniquely equipped to negotiate with the Hebrews' captors. After all, he had grown up as the adopted son of Pharaoh's daughter, learning Egyptian culture and customs as a palace insider. Now it was time for God to keep his promise once again: to set his people free and lead them to their new home.

As I've studied the Old Testament, I've noticed a pattern that seems to play out repeatedly across time and cultures—and remains valid today. People go from living in the truth of God's promise to falling away into sin and bondage, only to be pursued and rescued by God as he fulfills his redemptive promise time and time again. This cycle began with Adam and Eve in the Garden and was disrupted by their rebellious decision to bite off more than they could chew. But God didn't give up; he simply set into motion his redemptive plan for how to relate to his new human creations. Even after humanity blew it again, and the flood came to wipe out the wickedness and start over with Noah and his family, God has always been determined to lead his people to freedom.

It's in this context, then, in Egypt, that God reestablishes his commitment to his people, in no uncertain terms:

> Say to the Israelites: "I am the Lord, and I will bring you out from under the yoke of the Egyptians. I will free you from being slaves to them, and I will redeem you with an outstretched arm and with mighty acts of judgment. I will take you as my own people, and I will be your God."
>
> EXODUS 6:6-7, NIV

* * *

In order to appreciate how God's words, through Moses, were received by the people, we need to keep a few things in mind. First, as I've mentioned, they had been waiting on God for a *long, long time*—four hundred years long. To put that in perspective, it is equivalent to the *entire span* of US history, from the founding of Jamestown in 1607 to our present day. So when the Israelites heard that God had sent a deliverer, the skeptics among them probably thought, *Yeah, right . . . whatever.* It's like getting political speech fatigue during an election year, when all the candidates start sounding alike, regardless of their viewpoint. For many of the Israelites, Moses' words may have seemed like just more of the same.

On top of this skepticism, the people were probably fearful about the uncertainty that loomed ahead of them. If you study the book of Exodus, you see that many of the Hebrews were reluctant to follow Moses. They were afraid he was just stirring up more trouble for them. And don't forget that Moses didn't have such a great reputation. Granted, he was an Israelite by blood, but he had enjoyed a cushy upbringing in the Egyptian palace as the adopted son of Pharaoh's daughter, and then had spent the next forty years hiding in the desert to avoid capture and conviction for murder. On top of all that, he apparently stuttered, which didn't help him make his case to the people.

But even with all their doubts, fears, and uncertainties, the Israelites could not dismiss God's promises. His words got them dreaming again—a dangerous luxury for slaves. They began to foresee their future—a future filled with

> *Even with all their doubts, fears, and uncertainties, the Israelites could not dismiss God's promises. His words got them dreaming again.*

freedom and joy and the promise of a better life. Like most of us, they needed to see the hope in the journey—sort of like a vacation brochure—before they could take the first step.

We're not so different today. Maybe something in your life hasn't gone right and now you think your best days are behind you. You've stopped dreaming. You want to give up. You feel enslaved to hopelessness. But if you're going to experience the power of God's promises, you're going to have to dream again. You're going to have to face your dream killers. Here are three big ones:

1. *Unfulfilled expectations.* We all have times in our lives when our expectations of God seem to go unmet. We think we know how he should intervene in a situation or provide for our needs, and then he does it his way and in his own timing.

   Several years ago, when my dad was diagnosed with cancer, we not only did everything medically we could do for him, but we also prayed and trusted God for a miracle. After a two-and-a-half-year battle with the disease, my dad went to be with the Lord. At the time, it sure felt as if my hopes had been dashed because God had not chosen to heal my dad. But the truth is, God had something better planned for him. He rescued him from this earth and took him to heaven where there is no crying or pain.

Can you recall moments in your life when you've experienced this kind of disappointment—times when you've come up short, feeling empty or hurting? "Hope deferred makes the heart sick, but a dream fulfilled is a tree of life" (Proverbs 13:12).

The danger with this dream killer is that it tempts us to take matters into our own hands, to try to make things happen our way. And too many times it stops us dead in our tracks.

The Bible includes numerous stories about people who had to push through their unfulfilled expectations in order to discover what God had planned for them. Often they took matters into their own hands, with predictable results. For instance, God promised Abraham and his wife a son, but they felt that time was running out because of their advanced age. So when Sarah offered her maidservant, Hagar, to Abraham as a kind of surrogate mother, he agreed. And it worked—at least Hagar conceived a son by Abraham. But this wasn't what God had in mind, and their attempt to move things along backfired (Genesis 16).

Our way is never as good as God's way.

2. *Unrelenting doubt.* Most people battle doubts from time to time. Doubt usually takes root in our minds

when we allow the enemy of our souls to question what God has promised us. Satan would love nothing more than for us to buy into his lies about who we are and what God is doing in our lives. "You'll never amount to anything. You don't have what it takes. There's no way God is going to do anything for you. You've messed up way too many times." Satan knows that doubt is the opposite of faith. If he can get in our minds, he thinks he can kill God's dreams for us.

After thirty years of ministry, I still battle doubts. Having been a C student while growing up in a poor part of Baton Rouge, Louisiana, a state that typically ranks at or near the bottom on most educational lists, I still hear voices in my head that I'm not adequate for the job at hand. And every time I listen to those voices and doubt what God has accomplished in my life, it paralyzes the dream he placed in my heart.

To combat the enemy's lies, I put a verse on my bathroom mirror years ago so I would see it every day: "He has enabled us to be ministers of his new covenant. This is a covenant not of written laws, but of the Spirit. The old written covenant ends in death; but under the new covenant, the Spirit gives life" (2 Corinthians 3:6). I thank God that I am competent as a minister of the gospel, not because of what I have accomplished, but because of God's Spirit in me.

3. *Unchangeable circumstances.* This dream killer makes us want to give up. It's a faulty mentality that believes we've reached a point from which our lives can never change. We begin to believe there's no way we're getting out of Egypt. Our problems have all the power over us. We think, *It's too late now. Don't make it worse by hoping for something that can never happen.* We think it's over. But it's never over when we serve a God who can raise the dead. That's what Abraham reasoned when God asked him to kill his only heir, Isaac. Abraham knew God had promised to make him the father of many nations. "It was by faith that Abraham offered Isaac as a sacrifice when God was testing him. Abraham, who had received God's promises, was ready to sacrifice his only son, Isaac, even though God had told him, 'Isaac is the son through whom your descendants will be counted.' Abraham reasoned that if Isaac died, God was able to bring him back to life again" (Hebrews 11:17-19).

Nothing defeats a dream killer like focusing on God's promises. And that's what the children of Israel began to do. God's message stirred something deep inside them and they dared to dream again.

✳ ✳ ✳

You're probably aware of how their dreams came true. When God unleashed the horrific final plague—taking the lives of all firstborn sons in Egypt, unless the door-posts of their houses were marked with blood from a sacrificial lamb—thousands of Egyptians lost their lives, prompting Pharaoh to let the Hebrew people leave that very night. Of course, he later changed his mind and chased after them, but by then they had reached the Red Sea, which parted . . . and, well, you know the rest of the story.

What you may not know is how this event has been commemorated every year since that dramatic night when death "passed over" the Hebrew households and destroyed their enemies. To this day, the Jews celebrate Passover to remember what God did for them long ago and to celebrate God's plan for their lives today.

Like most cultural holidays, the celebration features traditional foods and customs, such as the breaking of the matzah, a kind of unleavened bread like a cracker, that reminds the Jewish people of how they had to leave their homes in a hurry—before the bread had a chance to rise—when God delivered them from Egypt. This unleavened bread served as a precursor, both to the manna that God provided for the Israelites in the desert and for the bread that Jesus blessed at the Last Supper, which he instructed

The wine also foreshadows the way in which God would ultimately save his people—through the sacrificial work of his Son, Jesus, on the cross.

his followers to use as a symbol of his body being broken for us.

At the heart of the Passover feast is a time of recognition and remembrance when four cups of wine are used to toast each of the four "I will" promises that God makes in Exodus 6:6-7 (which is also read at this time).

The richness of the wine contrasts dramatically with the bland matzah and provides a flavorful reminder of God's four promises. As a reminder of the Passover blood, the wine also foreshadows the way in which God would ultimately save his people—through the sacrificial work of his Son, Jesus, on the cross.

* * *

God not only rescued his people from bondage in Egypt, he also freed them from a slavery mind-set. The four million people that Moses led out of captivity had all grown up as slaves. They knew nothing about how to live as free men and women, how to take care of themselves, how to enjoy life without an overseer whipping them or working them until they dropped. But God promised to free them from the mind-set of enslavement.

That's why he provided the Israelites with so many laws and instructions covering every area of life, including personal hygiene, finances, parenting, and choosing a spouse. The book of Leviticus contains hundreds of these rules and regulations, not because God is a strict taskmaster who wants to make sure that everyone washes properly behind their ears, but because, at the time, his people didn't know how to live in true freedom. Living in bondage—to an evil master or to sin—will do that to you. So many people today seem to think of God as some sort of tax accountant who gets hung up on every single thing we do or don't do. But this perception has no basis. God gives us instructions for how to take care of ourselves—an owner's manual, if you will—because he knows us better than we know ourselves.

God promised to redeem his people "with an outstretched arm" and "mighty acts of judgment" (Exodus 6:6, NIV). He reaches down to us while we're enslaved and performs miracles that restore our worth and human dignity. God created us in his own divine image, and he wants that image to be reflected without obstruction or corruption. As the psalmist writes, "What are mere mortals that you should think about them, human beings that you should care for them? Yet you made them only a little lower than God and crowned them with glory and honor. You gave them charge of everything you made, putting all things under their authority" (Psalm 8:4-6).

People who have been slaves—subjected to abuse, mistreatment, and confinement—often don't know how to function as they were originally intended. When we find ourselves captive to our own selfish and sinful behavior, we lose sight of our purpose. But God has promised to redeem us, to reach down into the muddy pit where we've stumbled and fallen and lift us up again—just as he did with the people of Israel when he brought them out of captivity in Egypt.

Finally, God promised us a spiritual heritage of purpose and fulfillment. He promised that we would know him as our Lord and be part of his family. We belong. We're part of a community that knows and loves the Lord and wants to serve him. We're people making a difference, just as our Creator designed us to do. In light of

God has promised to redeem us, to reach down into the muddy pit where we've stumbled and fallen and lift us up again.

our awareness of our true identity as sons and daughters of the King, we find ourselves compelled to praise him, worship him, and serve him so that others may be set free as well.

In the ancient sacrament of Passover, we find a picture of God's heart for us that has never changed. What he promised to the people of Israel while they were captive in Egypt he still promises to people today who find themselves captive to addictions, vices, and hurtful behavior. God designed us to be free, to love him, to be in relationship with him, and to live out the fulfilling purpose for which he created us.

As you reflect on what God did for his people thousands of years ago, it's vitally important to realize that his promises remain alive to you today. Use this prayer to help you consider what it means for God to rekindle the embers of your dreams.

Lord, it's hard to remember sometimes that the dramatic way you liberated your children in Egypt is the same way you're liberating me today. Help me to face my dream killers and to use the power of your promises as my weapon. I want to hope again, to trust you with my future, to dream again. Breathe new life into me, God, so that I can experience the fullness of all your promises. Amen.

CHAPTER THREE

FREEDOM
IN CHRIST

All of God's promises have been fulfilled

in Christ with a resounding "Yes!"

2 CORINTHIANS 1:20

BY THE TIME FIFTEEN CENTURIES had passed since the children of Israel crossed the Red Sea, their dreams once again lay dormant, and God's promises were preserved only as well-worn stories for the annual Passover celebration. Once again, the people were in need of hope. Conquered by the Romans, they clung to their national identity and looked for a long-promised deliverer—someone like Moses of old—who would lead them to freedom. And now the rumors had begun to circulate about a teacher named Jesus, one of their own from Nazareth, who was doing and saying some incredible things. Could he really be the Messiah? We can only imagine what it must have been like . . .

A cluster of women sat knitting in a village on the outskirts of Jerusalem. The morning sun dodged behind a solitary cloud, giving a brief respite from the heat that would soon be absorbed by every clay structure on the square. Somewhere, a donkey brayed, and children laughed from a nearby terrace.

The women had been working for only a few hours, but already Judith's fingers were tired from the repetitive movements that her mother and grandmother made look so easy.

"Have you heard about this man they say has come back from the dead?" asked one of Judith's cousins. "He has many followers because of all the miracles he performed, but the Romans had him crucified like a common criminal."

"Hush your gossiping tongue," said one of the older women. "You never know where Roman spies are lurking."

"No, Ramah," said Hannah, another of the older women. "It is good to speak of this man, Jesus. My brother encountered him in the most amazing way, and his life has changed so dramatically that I almost cannot recognize him. He says that Jesus is truly the promised Messiah."

"Zacchaeus has changed? Surely you're joking," said Ramah harshly. "That little weasel is in cahoots with the Romans to steal our money! Can a jackal ever really change?"

"I'll admit he has not been a very honorable man," Hannah replied. "But that's what makes his transformation so remarkable. When this Jesus came to a nearby village a while back, Zacchaeus hid up high in a sycamore tree so that he could see above the crowd to see Jesus as he passed by. And you know what? Jesus stopped and came over to the very tree where my brother was hiding and told him to come down. And then he announced that he would eat the evening meal with Zacchaeus! Ever since that day, my brother has been returning the tax monies he

stole from people, and he is about to give up his
tax collecting business to become a craftsman.
Until Jesus was arrested, Zacchaeus followed him
around, absorbing every word he said."

"So what does he say about Jesus dying and
coming back from the grave?" asked Judith, clearly
fascinated by the older woman's story.

Hannah stopped her knitting and put down
the thin, camel-bone needles. She wiped her
brow on her forearm and adjusted the light linen
kerchief that held her hair away from her face. No
one made a sound as they waited to hear what she
would say next.

"Well," Hannah said, "Zacchaeus hasn't seen
him up close yet, but he and some of his good
friends saw Jesus on the beach not long ago, eating
with a group of his closest followers."

"And how is he so sure this was really the
same man who was put to death?" asked Ramah.
"There are no ghosts, you know."

"No," said Hannah. "My brother swears that
Jesus is the Messiah and he is alive again. He said
he would know the sound of his voice anywhere."

"So what happened to Jesus?" asked Judith.
"Has he started teaching and preaching again?"

"He told his disciples that he must leave
again," she said. "And they must wait in Jerusalem
for the promise of God to be fulfilled. Jesus said

that he wants all people to know the truth about his Father's love, even the Gentiles."

A slight gasp echoed among the women. There was silence—not even Ramah could bring herself to comment—and soon the women returned to their knitting. Judith wondered, *Can it be true? Could this Jesus really be the Son of God come to save the world? Could he really know everything about me and still love me?*

❉ ❉ ❉

After Moses died, the people of Israel drifted from God and began worshiping false gods and man-made idols. The cycle of faith—from living in the truth of God's promise . . . to falling away into sin and bondage . . . to God's pursuit and rescue . . . to living in the truth of God's promise—continued through the time of the judges and kings and various battles, both inside and outside the nation of God's chosen people.

We see this pattern of promise→bondage→rescue throughout the rest of the Old Testament. The initial revelation of God's promises in the four cups simply didn't work, because humanity did not yet have the living Spirit of God to empower them from within. They simply had the external law.

By the time of Jesus' birth in Bethlehem, the nation of Israel was once again in bondage, this time under Roman rule. You may remember that many Jews expected the

coming Messiah, who had been prophesied many generations before, to be a political revolutionary—someone
who would unite and inspire the Jewish tribes and defeat
the Roman emperor and his generals. Someone who
would restore Israel to her prior greatness and fulfill the
Scriptures of old. Someone
who would save the people.

Jesus came to fulfill the promises that God made to his people. But he also extended the four cups of promise to all future generations.

Of course, Jesus was not
an earthly king and hadn't
intended to be. He came
not to rule by earthly stan-
dards of power and wealth
and authority, but with the
full authority of his heav-
enly Father. Jesus came not to save the Jewish people from
Roman rule, but to save all people from the crushing
weight of their sin.

Jesus came to fulfill the promises that God made to
his people. And he not only fulfilled the promise to free
God's people from oppression and rescue them from slavery, and to stretch out his hand and do mighty works, but
he also extended the four cups of promise to all future
generations, through what has come to be called the Great
Commission.

But the Great Commission wasn't something *new*. It
was the same set of promises that God made to his people at
the time of the Exodus. In a sense, the Great Commission
symbolizes a passing of the torch. God fulfilled his promise

to his people by sending his Son to earth to atone for our sin. Jesus extended the promise to his followers by sending them out to all people everywhere to share the gospel. In his own place, he sent the Holy Spirit to guide, comfort, and lead us as we pursue this endeavor and live out our corporate mission (our "co-mission," to put it more accurately) and our individual purposes. As we'll see, the Great Commission represents a *culmination* of the four cups of promise carried to us through the centuries in the Passover Seder celebration.

✳ ✳ ✳

If we use the four cups of the Seder to help us compare God's promises in Exodus 6 with Christ's commissioning of the disciples in Matthew 28, the parallels become even clearer.

The first cup, the Cup of Sanctification, is based on God's promise, "I will bring you out from under the yoke of the Egyptians" (Exodus 6:6, NIV). In the Great Commission, Christ's first directive is about going to rescue people who are still lost in their sins. We do this through evangelism, when we share the message of how Christ's death and resurrection paid the price for our sins so that we can be restored to a right relationship with God, which he intended from the start.

Sanctification (being set apart as special and holy to God) goes hand in hand with evangelism (welcoming others into God's family and helping them see how God has set them apart for his purpose). Although we aren't slaves in Egypt, we all struggle with some form of bondage that prevents us from living freely the way our Father intended. Even more important, Christ has rescued us from the yoke, or weight, of sin that would otherwise separate us from God forever. The good news of the first cup is that God sent his only Son, Jesus, to perform the ultimate rescue—recovering and restoring the lost, no matter who or where they are.

The second cup, the Cup of Deliverance, is based on God's promise, "I will free you from being slaves" (Exodus 6:6, NIV). God promised his people that he would not only bring them physically out of Egypt, but he would also free them from the slavery mind-set that had become second nature to them. The parallel in the Great Commission is that we are to teach others to know the truth—about God, about themselves, about why they were created. As we recognize our weaknesses, our sinful mistakes, and our need for forgiveness, we need to know that our Savior offers us a new way of living that can free us from enslavement of sin. Deliverance—overcoming the mind-set of slavery to sin— is often a lifelong battle. And it's a battle we can win only by relying on Jesus day by day and moment by moment.

At Church of the Highlands, we often think of this cup as the "cup of pastoral care," which is obviously near and dear to my heart. One of the great privileges of my role as a pastor is the opportunity to *shepherd* the souls that God brings into the flock of our church. It's rarely easy, because life is messy; but it's rewarding beyond measure. Caring for people is a huge part of my individual purpose and intrinsic to the way God made me. I want everyone to know the loving care and infinite kindness and goodness of our heavenly Father, the one true Source of all life and love.

> As we recognize our weaknesses, our sinful mistakes, and our need for forgiveness, our Savior offers us a new way of living that can free us from enslavement of sin.

The third cup, the Cup of Redemption, is based on God's promise, "I will redeem you with an outstretched arm and with mighty acts of judgment" (Exodus 6:6, NIV). This is God's promise to redeem his people, restore them to greatness, and lead them to their true purpose in life. In the Great Commission, Jesus expresses this redemptive promise by telling us to *make disciples* from new believers. We're not only to teach them the truth about God's Word, about who Jesus is, and about God's love and grace, but we're also to help them live out the truth in their own lives. We set a good example and practice what we preach. We equip people to live the new life of freedom, discover their real purpose, and then put it into practice as they serve others.

The fourth cup, the Cup of Praise, is based on God's promise, "I will take you as my own people, and I will be your God" (Exodus 6:7, NIV). As we live in community with other believers, we naturally begin to praise God for his faithfulness, as expressed in the Great Commission: "Be sure of this: I am with you always, even to the end of the age" (Matthew 28:20). If ever there was a reason to be thankful and praise God, it's for the unfathomable gift of Christ's love and his sacrificial death on the cross for us. Through his example, we die to our own selfish, petty desires and discover the joy of living for a larger purpose.

Here's a simple prayer to guide you as you reflect on this chapter:

> *Heavenly Father, thank you for desiring to know me and to have a close relationship with me. I'm so grateful you were willing to send your Son to be human and to bridge the gap between my sinful nature and your holy one. I'm amazed at how your timeless message echoes across all the pages of the Bible, from the four "I wills" in Exodus to the Great Commission in the Gospels. Thank you that your promises are the same yesterday, today, and forever. Amen.*

CHAPTER FOUR

THE CUP OF SANCTIFICATION

I will bring you out from under the

yoke of the Egyptians.

EXODUS 6:6, NIV

LIKE MOST COUPLES when they marry, Tammy and I received many place settings and serving pieces of our beautiful wedding china. Even though I don't know much about fine china, I know how special ours is to us—so special that it stays in its own antique china cabinet. Whenever we use it, we always take extra care to wash and dry the pieces by hand before returning them to the security of the china cabinet.

Another way to describe our china is that it has been *sanctified*. I know that sounds like a religious or theological word, kind of abstract and conceptual, like something floating on the clouds near heaven that we can never attain. But all it really means is that our china is special and unique and has been set aside for a particular purpose.

Many people seem to assume that sanctification means "righteous" or "perfect." Although this association makes sense, it's technically inaccurate. When something is sanctified, it's not necessarily perfect; it simply means it has been set aside or designated for a particular, unique purpose. Our wedding china isn't perfect; it's just set aside for special occasions and important family dinners. Our church sanctuary isn't perfect; it's just a building set aside as a place to gather and worship. A marriage isn't perfect; but it's a relationship that has been set apart from all other relationships by a commitment between two people who agree to "forsake all others" and pledge their fidelity and intimacy solely to each other.

I like to use these examples to define *sanctification*

because everyone understands that wedding china, church buildings, and marriages aren't perfect, but they are called out and set aside from others of their kind.

It's important to understand what sanctification *is* and *isn't* if we're going to grasp the scope and magnitude of God's first promise. He wants to *set us apart*. Because to him we're special and he has never created—nor will he ever create—anyone exactly like you or me. We're not perfect—we're well aware of that—but we were designed to be set apart for God's purpose.

✳ ✳ ✳

At some point we've all found ourselves in bondage to something, living common lives with no purpose. We've settled for less, resigned ourselves to mediocrity, and started to believe we're nothing special. This path always leads to slavery—which is a life we were never intended to live.

> *Once we, too, were foolish and disobedient. We were misled and became slaves to many lusts and pleasures. Our lives were full of evil and envy, and we hated each other. But—*
>
> *"When God our Savior revealed his kindness and love, he saved us, not because of the righteous things we had done, but because of his mercy. He washed away our sins, giving us a new birth and new life through the Holy Spirit."*
>
> TITUS 3:3-5

When God promised to bring his people out of their captivity in Egypt, he provided a way, through the blood of the sacrificial lamb, even when Pharaoh stubbornly refused. God made the same kind of promise to us and provided a way out of our bondage to sin through the sacrifice of Jesus. Even though the enemy of our souls does everything he can to thwart us, we are no longer enslaved to sin.

To this day, during Passover celebrations, the Jewish people celebrate the fact that God had a plan to get them out of slavery. They worship the God who heard their cry and rescued them from bondage. The first cup of Passover honors this foundational promise that God wants his people to experience salvation so they can live the life of freedom that he always intended for them.

This desire to set people free from bondage remains at the center of God's heart. He sees every person on earth as his child, though some are still lost. Throughout Jesus' ministry on earth, he made it clear that his mission was to seek and save the lost (Luke 19:10). When God sees his children who are still enslaved to sin, he wants them free. He wants us out of the muddy pit where we're eating pig food like the Prodigal Son. He wants to lift us up and set us apart (sanctify us) from the world. He offers to save us if we'll let him.

My own story of salvation surely bears this out. It's not a hair-raising tale of a reformed drug addict or serial killer, but my life before I encountered Christ was no less destructive. I was in my own kind of bondage, a slippery, muddy pit from which there seemed no escape.

At an early age, I sensed that my life had a purpose. But like most people, I struggled to discern what it was. Even though I grew up in the church and never missed a Sunday service, God wasn't real to me. I went through the motions of trying to "find" him and find out what he had in store for me, but I always came up empty. I wasn't particularly talented or smart, and I certainly wasn't popular or a natural leader. One of the most painful experiences of my childhood was being tied to a fence by a group of bullies and ridiculed as a loser.

> *When God sees his children who are still enslaved to sin, he wants them free. He wants us out of the muddy pit where we're eating pig food like the Prodigal Son.*

Though I was soon set free from the fence, the bondage in my soul became more real and dangerous the older I got. In contrast to the church, which seemed fake and religious, the world seemed real and appealing, with so much more to offer. I felt as if I had developed a double life: going through the motions at church on Sunday after exploring the adult vices on Friday and Saturday nights that many teens find so appealing.

Then, when I was fifteen, a friend invited me to a new church. I wasn't interested. My friend had recently become a devout Christian, and it seemed he now spent all his time reading the Bible. But when he told me there were a lot of pretty girls in the youth group, it was reason enough for me to check it out.

It was there that the gospel of Jesus penetrated my heart for the first time. I'm sure I had heard the truth before, but this time it got through to me. Still, when they gave an altar call, I didn't respond, because I didn't want anyone to know that I wasn't already a Christian.

At first, I thought of it as a "rededication," but I knew in my heart that what I'd had before wasn't real, and that this time I was having a genuine, first-time conversion experience.

I went home that night under deep conviction and asked God to "give me another chance." I got on my knees, laid my arms across my bed, and told the Lord that if he would forgive me, he would never find a more devoted follower—I would give him everything. When I woke up the next morning, I was on fire for God. I knew he had saved me and I felt totally free. I had been given a fresh start.

❊ ❊ ❊

Even with my newfound zeal, I still had a long way to go. I immediately joined the youth group at the new church and got involved in the small groups they had for teens. It was there that I not only had the chance to share my struggles and ask questions, but I was also surrounded by people who encouraged me to grow.

One of the steps they prompted me to take was to share my real life with my parents. Until then, I had successfully concealed all my wild living from my parents. They thought I was a pure-hearted, godly little boy.

That was a tough conversation. My mom cried as I told the truth about what I'd been doing. It was my dad's response that surprised me. He was smiling—not because of what I had revealed, but because he knew that something significant was happening in my life.

> *Something miraculous happened in that confession that freed me from my past once and for all. I knew God had forgiven me.*

That conversation took place more than thirty-five years ago, but I remember it as if it were yesterday. Something miraculous happened in that confession that freed me from my past once and for all. I knew God had forgiven me. His presence in my life was different from anything I'd ever experienced.

The years that followed turned out to be the most significant of my life. I served the Lord with my whole heart and got involved in everything the church was doing. The summer after I graduated from high school, I attended our church's annual summer camp. The guest speaker that year ministered with the gift of prophecy—something I had not heard before.

One night during the evening service, in an open-air, outdoor pavilion, the speaker called me out of the crowd and asked me to come forward. He said he had a "word" for me from God. I was terrified and exhilarated at the same time.

When I reached the platform, the speaker put his hand on my shoulder and said that one day my life would impact thousands of people. He told me to look up at the stars—just like God had done with Abraham—and said, "That's how big of an impact God wants to have through you." He then asked if he could pray for me and told me to lift my hands.

As he prayed, something happened that I cannot explain to this day. Every joint in my hands and fingers popped and seemed to grow in length. I felt the tangible presence of God that night. I didn't know exactly what it meant, but I knew that God had a plan for my life. He was setting me apart for something special. I was drinking from the Cup of Sanctification. I realize that not everyone will encounter God in this way, but he still wants to reveal himself to you and set you apart for something special.

> *I felt the tangible presence of God that night. I didn't know exactly what it meant, but I knew that God had a plan for my life.*

* * *

The enemy of your soul also has something planned for you. He wants you to stay under his control, feeling as if there is no way out.

Perhaps you find yourself in some type of bondage

right now. It could be an addiction or a secret habit that you cling to. It could be an unhealthy relationship or an obsession with appearing successful in the eyes of others. Regardless of what holds you down, you find yourself a slave to something that you know is not why you were created, and God seems a million miles away.

God is not far from you. In fact, he has made a promise to you and is always pursuing you. When you find yourself wondering why you're even here, it's because of the sense of destiny he placed in your heart. When you feel curious about what you're supposed to do with your life and what difference it will make, that's God calling you to drink from the Cup of Sanctification. He wants to quench your thirst for more, for a purpose, for something larger and more meaningful than you can imagine.

> *From one man he made every nation of men, that they should inhabit the whole earth; and he determined the times set for them and the exact places where they should live. God did this so that men would seek him and perhaps reach out for him and find him, though he is not far from each one of us.*
> ACTS 17:26-27, NIV

God put you on planet Earth at this exact time and place so that you can fulfill the purpose for which you were created. And the only way for you to find the answer is to come to him. He is the only one with the book on your life.

You saw me before I was born. Every day of my life was recorded in your book. Every moment was laid out before a single day had passed.

PSALM 139:16

When you earnestly want to know your purpose and seek God for the answer, you'll discover he's very near. In fact, he's been there all along. You just need to drink from the Cup of Sanctification and experience real salvation.

But maybe this step seems difficult to you. Maybe, like so many people, you haven't experienced salvation because you think God wants something from you first; that you have to get some things right in your life before God will listen to you. Drinking from this cup is not hard—it's actually the easiest thing you'll ever do. But when you're in bondage, lost and far away from your true home, it can feel complicated.

If religions have one thing in common, it's that they require us to *do something* to get to God. All except Christianity. So many people, including many Christians, believe that God requires us to make changes before we can approach him. But that's not true. We don't get our lives together in order to get to God. We go to God to get our lives together! So what are we supposed to do?

The answer is in God's first cup of promise. He said, "I will bring you out."

Let me explain.

✳ ✳ ✳

Sometimes we're tempted to try to earn our way into the abundant life. But God's Word is undeniably clear that, no matter how hard we try, no matter how much we do or how long we do it, it will never be enough. We simply cannot *earn* God's favor. Even better . . . *we don't have to.*

The Bible tells us, "God saved you by his grace when you believed. And you can't take credit for this; it is a gift from God" (Ephesians 2:8). We don't have to work to curry favor with God. The moment we believed and committed our lives to him, he gave us the best present we could ever hope to receive—adoption into the family of God. We can't take credit for our salvation, because there's nothing we've done or can do to make God love us. He already does.

"Wait a minute," you might say. "Doesn't the Bible tell us to love others and serve them and *do* stuff?" Yes, it does. But all that comes *after* we are sanctified, once we've been separated from the old life we were in.

> *Work hard to show the results of your salvation, obeying God with deep reverence and fear. For God is working in you, giving you the desire and the power to do what pleases him.*
> PHILIPPIANS 2:12-13

Once God becomes the Lord of your life, he begins working in your heart to give you both the *desire* and the *power* to change. Not before. A lot of change will happen after you've been set free, but you don't change in order to become free. Salvation is a gift.

So how do you get started? First, realize that God is pursuing you. Jesus says, "You didn't choose me. I chose you" (John 15:16). In the Exodus story, God says to Moses, "I have certainly seen the oppression of my people in Egypt. I have heard their cries of distress because of their harsh slave drivers. Yes, I am aware of their suffering. So I have come down to rescue them from the power of the Egyptians and lead them out of Egypt" (Exodus 3:7-8).

God has never stopped thinking about you. He has seen your wandering, and your suffering, and he wants you back home. So what does he do? He leads you out and all you have to do is follow.

When you follow someone, you give up control of where you're going, and you trust that the leader knows the way. If you were lost in the woods and ran across some experienced hikers who knew their way around, they could simply say, "Follow us and we'll show you the way," and you could decide either to stay lost or take them up on their offer. That's the easy part. But once you decide to leave behind the place where you were lost, the trail back to civilization might include some rough terrain, some hills and some valleys, and you might have to work to make your way back. But you trust yourself to the leader, and off you go.

When it comes to living life with God, you have to decide to leave behind your old life in order to follow him to the land he has promised you. And the road ahead may include some rough terrain, some hills and some valleys. But when you put your trust in God, you bind yourself to his promise that he will lead you out.

How do we take that first sip from the Cup of Sanctification? In a word: *surrender*. Give up control of your life and turn it over to God. He knows everything that holds you back, he knows the path that lies ahead, and he has sent one greater than Moses to lead you out. All you have to do is follow.

If you have never made Jesus the Lord of your life, or if you've wandered far from God, here is a simple prayer you can pray to completely surrender your life to him. May God bless you as you drink from the Cup of Sanctification.

> *Father God, thank you for loving me the way you do. For so long I have been wandering around far from you, living my life my own way. Please forgive me. Today I respond to your Spirit, who is leading me home, by giving you my life. Today I receive what Jesus did for me on the cross and I receive the free gift of salvation. Be the Lord of my life. Thank you for setting me free. I'm ready to follow you, and I trust that you know the way. Amen.*

CHAPTER FIVE

THE CUP OF DELIVERANCE

I will . . . rescue you

from your slavery.

EXODUS 6:6

IMAGINE THAT YOU and your family have been impris-
oned for years; so many years, in fact, that you have no
memory other than being in chains and forced to follow
orders from your captors. Now imagine that you and your
family and all the people like you—approximately four
million others—are suddenly released and forced to create
a new life.

No problem, right? It sounds simple enough. Being
free is surely better than being enslaved. But curiously
enough, for the Israelites fleeing Egypt, God's dramatic
emancipation left them with a new set of problems. Not
only did they end up wandering around for forty years
looking for a new home, but they also had to learn how
to be a free society all over
again.

This phenomenon is not
as unusual as it may sound.
Of the people in the United
States who are incarcerated
and then released, almost
half will return to prison
within three years of gaining their freedom.[1] Why and
how they return is certainly a combination of many complex variables, and comparing them to a people who were
enslaved in a foreign culture is not comparing apples to
apples. Still, there's something about our human nature
that learns to adapt to our surroundings, no matter how
painful or difficult they may be. Then, when circumstances

> We can be free spiritually,
> committed to following Jesus
> and living for God, and yet
> still act like slaves to old habits
> and sinful behaviors.

change, we often find it hard to know how to function without the familiarity of our prior captivity, and we may go back to those enslaving habits.

This tendency to need help reacclimating to a new life explains the message behind God's second promise to his people, represented by the second cup: "I . . . will rescue you from your slavery." At first, it may seem redundant. Why would God promise to deliver the children of Israel from being slaves *after* they were already set free from their oppression in Egypt? Because even though they weren't slaves anymore, they still thought and acted like slaves. The same is true for you and me today. We can be free spiritually, committed to following Jesus and living for God, and yet still act like slaves to old habits and sinful behaviors.

Even after the children of Israel left the land of Egypt, there was still a little bit of Egypt left in them. They were free people, en route to the land God had promised to them as their new home, but they still had a slave mentality and still acted like slaves. They had a wrong view of themselves, a distrustful view of God, and a skeptical view of the future. To put it bluntly, their thinking was messed up!

Many people today still have messed-up thinking. Many believers are en route to heaven but are still plagued by selfish habits, secret addictions, and sinful attitudes. Just like the Israelites, they need the Cup of Deliverance. If they're ever going to move into the future that God has for them, they need to be delivered from an old mind-set that clings to the past.

* * *

Deliverance. For a certain generation, it sounds like something out of an *Exorcist*-type horror movie or a wilderness scene in backwoods Arkansas—both equally scary. But despite what we may associate with the word, deliverance isn't just for people with demons. Deliverance is for anyone still struggling with their sinful nature. It's for people whose past keeps limiting their future. In other words, it's for *everyone*.

Deliverance is different from salvation. Salvation takes care of our eternity; deliverance determines our quality of life while still on earth. Salvation, the first cup, is instant. Deliverance, the second cup, is a process. When God saves us, he forgives everything we've ever done, but often our habits, attitudes, and sins linger on. And for most of us, we're still haunted by memories and pains of the past. But God didn't save us only to have us settle for less than his best.

The Cup of Deliverance closes the door on yesterday once and for all. How? By helping us become whole and complete people, delivered from our past enslavements.

To better understand the Cup of Deliverance, think of it this way. Just as God is a trinity comprising Father, Son, and Holy Spirit, people are triune beings made up of body, soul, and spirit. This triunity makes sense because we're created in God's image. When we get saved, God completely cleanses us spiritually. Our spirit is then empowered by the Holy Spirit to begin the process of regeneration, a transformation of our spirit, which then affects and changes the other two parts of our being.

Despite being saved, however, we often cling to our old, familiar ways, instead of experiencing the deliverance and spiritual transformation that God wants to complete in our lives. We let our bodily appetites and fleshly desires continue to drive our thinking and behavior. We allow our souls—our mind, will, and emotions—to be clouded by past circumstances and injuries. Like the Israelites coming out of bondage, we don't grasp the extent of the freedom we've received through salvation. We remain broken and fragmented.

> *The Cup of Deliverance closes the door on yesterday once and for all.*

In mathematics, the term *integer* refers to a whole number (not a fraction). It comes from the same root as the word *integrity*, which also means wholeness or completeness. When we lack integrity, we don't feel whole. Something is missing; we're not complete. Sin often erodes our integrity and fragments our lives into secret behaviors and deceptive attitudes. We end up less than whole, frustrated by the battle within us.

Sin, as you might know, is simply missing the mark

of God's standard, which is perfect holiness. More practically, I'm defining sin as simply the wrong choices we make based on our ingrained beliefs, attitudes, habits, and behaviors. It includes ongoing struggles, which we often label as addictions, as well as more opportunistic moments when we take shortcuts rather than choose what God wants us to do.

> *Salvation ignites our spiritual transformation, renewing and empowering our spirit, and recalibrating it to God's original purpose.*

Salvation ignites our spiritual transformation, renewing and empowering our spirit, and recalibrating it to God's original purpose. Our spirit was designed to influence the other two parts—the body and soul. But in order for this to happen, the body and soul must go through a cleansing process and submit to the work of the Holy Spirit in us. Basically, we have to learn how God intended for us to live rather than continue in the sinful ways that have become our default mode.

✳ ✳ ✳

So how do we allow God's Spirit to transform us into truly free people? Sin can be so discouraging because its cancerous tentacles try to infiltrate our lives at every turn, no matter how hard we try to fight it. The apostle Paul makes this struggle clear when he writes, "I find this law at work: Although I want to do good, evil is right there with me. For in my inner being I delight in God's law; but I see another law at work in me, waging war against the law of my mind and making me a prisoner of the law of sin at work within me. What a wretched man I am!" (Romans 7:21-24, NIV).

Battling sin can be so frustrating because we know we shouldn't have done it and we want help, but we feel as if we can't let anyone know. We worry, "What will they think of me? What kind of Christian am I to have done something like this? How can anyone else help me anyway?" Then the devil begins to torment us and accuse, "Who do you think you are? What a loser! You're never going to stop doing this."

But this simply isn't true. We can be free if we're willing to follow the guidelines that God has provided for our best interests. It's a process that we can't achieve alone. It requires *community* within the body of Christ, the church. Though there are various ways that a group of believers can help one another through the process of deliverance, it's often most effective when practiced deliberately.

At Church of the Highlands, one of our most popular types of small group is what we call our LIFE groups: Living In Freedom Everyday. These small groups systematically take people through a process of dealing with the various struggles that are holding them back. We usually focus on three main areas: sins, wounds, and curses. Let's consider each of these and the way God's cup of deliverance addresses them.

* * *

In our LIFE groups, we examine our sins as exposed through our attitudes, habits, and addictions. We often discover false beliefs within our attitudes, which then affect every other area of our lives. We may not even realize how ingrained false beliefs or deceptive ideas can be. Similarly, we may have habits that expose us to unnecessary risks for sinful behavior or that simply don't draw us closer to God.

Now, let's talk about addictions for a moment, in case you think this one doesn't apply to you. It may be tempting to think that addictions only enslave people who can't stop drinking or gambling or having illicit sex. These are the kinds of big-ticket items we tend to think of as addictions. But actually, an addiction is anything we do that we don't want to do but we can't stop doing. It is any ingrained pattern that pulls us to false idols to escape our pain.

It's easy to be arrogant or judgmental about somebody else's addictions but to make exceptions for your own—or even to be completely blind to your own. Maybe you don't do crack, but you think nothing of spending five hours a day on Facebook. You may not smoke, but you don't think twice about overeating at every meal. You've never gambled, but you're glued to the television every night and you can't stop checking for e-mail, text, and Twitter updates on your phone. Addictions aren't just recovery-group issues. But they are life-altering.

Let me ask you a different question: What are the things in your life that have control over you? Be honest with yourself. Maybe it will be easier to identify your addictions if you consider their usual cycle.

At first, it's just something we do, but then it becomes a part of our identity. We see ourselves a certain way, even if we don't let the full weight of it sink in. "I'm a workaholic" or a "sports freak" or a "fashionista"—we have all kinds of ways of joking about our addictions and acting like they're no big deal. But Satan wants us to internalize these behaviors and attitudes. He wants us to feel as if they're essential to our identity and well-being.

> *It's easy to be arrogant or judgmental about somebody else's addictions, but to make exceptions for your own—or even to be completely blind to your own.*

Part of an addiction's power is that when you try to quit, you fail. You cut back on working overtime for a week but then find yourself creeping back toward twelve-hour days. You stick to your budget all month and then splurge on a new pair of shoes. You eat healthy foods at mealtimes, but sneak candy bars in between. Pretty soon, you feel hopeless about ever living without your addictive crutch.

You can also recognize your addictions by the way you protect them. Any threat to your addiction becomes a threat to you. People who try to help you or hold you accountable feel like enemies. Slowly but surely, you begin to lose your life to the pull of your addiction. You worry or feel guilty or ashamed about your secret, but then those emotions trigger your need for the comfort of your favorite means of escape, and the addictive cycle starts all over again.

This is the enemy's ultimate goal: to rob you of a joyful, fulfilled life and keep you from being effective. He comes to steal, kill, and destroy (John 10:10). Left unchecked, your addictions will keep you on a treadmill of frustration and mediocrity, never growing into your God-given potential. They become your master and you remain a slave. But that's not where God wants to leave you. As Paul writes, "'Everything is permissible for me'—but I will not be mastered by anything" (1 Corinthians 6:12, NIV).

Next, our LIFE groups focus on wounds. We define wounds as negative events that have happened to us—usually, what others have done to us, things over which we had little or no control. This may include childhood abuse, harsh words of criticism and judgment from others, betrayal by a spouse or other close loved one, rejection and abandonment, and all the other losses that often leave us beaten and bruised.

Though we may have tried to forgive, it's often easier to cling to anger and bitterness. Here again, our enemy is looking for a foothold, and relational injuries often open the door to him. Throughout Scripture, we're reminded that anger gives the devil a doorway into our lives. "'Don't

sin by letting anger con-
trol you.' Don't let the sun
go down while you are
still angry, for anger gives
a foothold to the devil"
(Ephesians 4:26-27).

*Though we may have tried to
forgive, it's often easier to cling
to anger and bitterness. Here
again, our enemy is looking for
a foothold.*

The third area we focus
on involves curses, which we
define as the plan of attack the enemy has for us. Curses are
the specific strategies the devil wants to use to take us down
and ruin our lives. Whether we're aware of it or not, we
have an enemy intent on undermining the life God wants
us to live. This enemy studies us and looks for opportune
times to attack.

Like the deadliest stealth sniper, he waits for us each
day, eager to shoot us down with his lies. If we don't watch
for him and arm ourselves with God's truth, the enemy
will succeed. Throughout God's Word, we're warned to
pay attention and be on guard against the devil's snares.
"Stay alert! Watch out for your great enemy, the devil. He
prowls around like a roaring lion, looking for someone to
devour" (1 Peter 5:8).

✳ ✳ ✳

God has promised us the Cup of Deliverance so that we
can overcome all obstacles. We can be delivered and live
in the joy of true freedom. Over the years, as thousands
of people have participated in our LIFE groups, here's

what we've discovered. When people confront the past—their sins, wounds, and curses—they experience amazing joy, freedom, and spiritual growth. They move from just the assurance of their salvation to an experience of divine deliverance.

God has promised us the Cup of Deliverance so that we can overcome all obstacles. We can be delivered and live in the joy of true freedom.

How? One of the best tools for deliverance is *confession*. When we confess to God, we have immediate assurance of his forgiveness. "If we confess our sins to him, he is faithful and just to forgive us our sins and to cleanse us from all wickedness" (1 John 1:9).

It seems as if confessing our sins to God would be enough, right? But he adds another piece to the deliverance puzzle: *confessing our sins to one another.* "Confess your sins to each other and pray for each other so that you may be healed" (James 5:16). Confessing to God takes care of the past—it takes care of what happened. But confessing to another person helps it not to happen again.

That's why, in order to drink from the Cup of Deliverance, you need at least one other follower of Christ involved, someone who loves God and loves you. When you confess your struggles with sin to another person, it brings a certain level of accountability. It's like when I'm trying to exercise and work out regularly. I'm more successful when I have a workout partner that I've agreed to meet at the gym. I'm much more inclined to go if I know my friend will be at the gym waiting for me. If you know that someone is going to check in with you and ask you what's really going on, it helps you think twice before following old habits.

There's also a miraculous part to confession and deliverance. When God designed us, he knew that half the battle for us would just be telling the truth and saying it to someone else. When we confess our faults, hurts, hang-ups, and missteps to another person, a spiritual dynamic takes place. Our confession to another person notifies the kingdom of darkness that we are ready for a change. When we verbalize our faults and invoke the name of the Lord over our situations, it overcomes the enemy of our soul. "They triumphed over him [the devil] by the blood of the Lamb and by the word of their testimony" (Revelation 12:11, NIV).

Another way to drink from the Cup of Deliverance and experience freedom is to invite Jesus to take his place as Lord over that area of your life. Why? Because any effort to break bad habits without a change of heart is a short-term fix at best. Actually, it's doomed to failure.

We need changed hearts—not just changed behavior. If our hearts change, our behavior will naturally change. But most of us don't want a changed life or a changed heart; we just want changed circumstances.

We don't want to stop overeating; we just want to be skinny. We don't want to stop overspending; we just want to be financially independent. We don't want to stop lusting, but we do want a good marriage.

The things that control us are not our real problem. Something much bigger is going on. The things that control us are only symptoms. The real disease is idolatry.

Don't let the word *idolatry* scare you off or cause you to underestimate its ability to infiltrate your life. It's not about having a satanic statue in your home to which you bow down. Idolatry is *anything* you allow to sit on the throne of your heart other than God—and we all do it from time to time. And when something sits on the throne of our hearts, we become a slave to it. Whatever sits on the throne of our hearts is what rules us.

✳ ✳ ✳

The practical application of this principle is simple: Every day, make Jesus Lord of your life. Every day, remove anything that is in competition for your heart. Every day, worship God—with your prayers, songs, and life. All that the children of Israel had to do to experience deliverance from being slaves was to give their hearts to God and his ways. God gave them all kinds of instructions and laws on how to live, in order to remind them of who they really were—sons and daughters of the King, not slaves of the enemy. After salvation, we must focus on new life rules that produce a new heart, new thinking, and new living.

The Old Testament laws that God gave to the Israelites

focused on living out the new rules externally. In the New Testament, as we've seen, the emphasis is on what happens *internally*, in our hearts. We see this explained very directly in a passage from Hebrews. Notice the way it echoes and reinforces the four "I wills" from Exodus 6:6-7.

> If the first covenant had been faultless, there would have been no need for a second covenant to replace it. But when God found fault with the people, he said:
> "The day is coming, says the Lord, when I will make a new covenant with the people of Israel and Judah.
> This covenant will not be like the one I made with their ancestors when I took them by the hand and led them out of the land of Egypt. They did not remain faithful to my covenant, so I turned my back on them, says the Lord.
> But this is the new covenant I will make with the people of Israel on that day, says the Lord: I will put my laws in their minds, and I will write them on their hearts. I will be their God, and they will be my people.
> And they will not need to teach their neighbors, nor will they need to teach their relatives, saying, 'You should know the Lord.' For everyone, from the least to the greatest, will know me already.
> And I will forgive their wickedness, and I will never again remember their sins."
>
> HEBREWS 8:7-12

Finally, please don't try to drink from the third or fourth cups of God's promises by skipping over or racing through this second cup. I tell you this mostly because you can't appreciate and experience the fullness of the third and fourth cups without experiencing the deliverance God has for you. You can't go on to tomorrow's work until you've settled yesterday's mess. You need to experience the healing that comes from a new completeness, a new wholeness, a new integrity, and that only comes from aligning your body, soul, and spirit with God's Spirit.

On the other hand, the enemy would love for you to stay stuck in the second cup. He wants you to spend the rest of your life looking in the rearview mirror instead of seeing the path God has set before you. If you're always plagued by your problems and your yesterdays, you won't grow into the fullness of your true purpose and place in God's Kingdom.

But God has provided the Cup of Deliverance for you, a gift of hope, redemption, and fulfillment. "Who will free me from this life that is dominated by sin and death? Thank God! The answer is in Jesus Christ our Lord" (Romans 7:24-25).

If you want to begin the process of drinking from the Cup of Deliverance, you can pray a simple prayer like this:

Father, I confess my sins to you and thank you for being faithful and just, and forgiving me of my sin and cleansing me from all unrighteousness. Lord, give me the courage and the wisdom to approach those people that love you and love me so that I can share my struggles and faults and experience healing. In every area, be the Lord of my life. Amen.

CHAPTER SIX

THE CUP OF REDEMPTION

I will redeem you with an outstretched arm

and with mighty acts of judgment.

EXODUS 6:6, NIV

WHEN I WAS YOUNG, I collected S&H Green Stamps. I have wonderful memories of taking the stamps we received at grocery stores, gas stations, and department stores and sticking them in the little booklets my mom gave to each of us kids. We would thumb through the catalogs for hours, ooh-ing and aah-ing over all the cool stuff we wanted to get with our stamps—bicycles, roller skates, guitars, you name it. Then when we had saved up enough stamps, we could redeem them—trading them in for that special item.

Saving and trading my Green Stamps for toys provided me a clear understanding of the words *redeem* and *redemption*. Even though I grew up in the church and probably heard the words dozens of times, what made an impression was being able to get something back for all those little pale green squares.

Redeem simply means to buy back or to cash in the value of something in order to receive something else. If you look it up in a dictionary, you'll find that it also means to win back, to free someone or something from what distresses or harms them, to liberate them from captivity by paying a ransom, to reform and restore. When God redeems us, he pays for our debt of sin through the sacrifice of Jesus on the cross. In return, we can experience the freedom to do what he created us to do.

As we see with the children of Israel in Egypt, God was not only interested in saving them and delivering them from slavery, but he also had a plan for them. He wanted to redeem their past suffering and painful struggles by turning them into something that could make the people stronger, wiser, and more focused on their relationship with him.

The same is true for God's people today. Redemption means that God enables us to do what we're supposed to be doing. For the Israelites, it wasn't making bricks for Pharaoh in a mud pit. God freed them to live productive and fulfilled lives in the land of promise. Regardless of the modern mud pits in which we find ourselves, God promises to do the same for us.

＊ ＊ ＊

God created us for a specific purpose—a purpose he had in mind before the foundations of the world. In fact, he had good works in mind for us, and then he created us. "For we are God's handiwork, created in Christ Jesus to do good works, which God prepared in advance for us to do" (Ephesians 2:10, NIV). The word that is translated "workmanship" here is *poiema*, which is also where we get our words *poem* and *poetry*. We are the poem that God knew he wanted to write by creating us. As God redeems us, we become his "word made flesh," transformed to be more and more like Jesus.

> *Redemption means that God enables us to do what we're supposed to be doing.*

Our redemption is the essence of *discipleship*. God has

created us and calls us all to be students of Christ's, learning and growing to be closer to our Father through his Son. Often we mistakenly think that discipleship requires special training or a seminary degree. But discipleship is not about learning more stuff—it's about discovering and developing the reason why we were created, and then living it out.

When you go to college, you don't just learn whatever they happen to be teaching in whatever classroom you stumbled into that day. You go to certain classes that are in your degree field, the area that you feel called to work in when you finish college. The goal of life isn't just to learn—learning is important and lifelong—but the goal is to *apply* what you've learned. God wants you to do what he created you to do. And according to the promise made in the Cup of Redemption, he goes about redeeming you in two ways.

> *Discipleship is not about learning more stuff—it's about discovering and developing the reason why we were created, and then living it out.*

First, he does it "with an outstretched arm" (Exodus 6:6, NIV). Can't you just visualize him reaching down and pulling us up when we've fallen? I love this concept! God extends his arm toward us so that we can take his hand and get back on our feet. He humbles himself by moving in our direction, or as the psalmist says, "You stoop down to make me great" (Psalm 18:35, NIV).

Why does he have to stoop down? Because we've been convinced that we're not so great; and we've resigned ourselves to the fact that our lives will be ordinary at best. God sees greatness in his people. He knows it's there because he created us and put it there. He sees greatness in *you* that you don't even see in yourself. God wants to help you discover what you were made to do and experience the fulfillment that comes from that.

I certainly didn't see greatness in myself. I was an average, C-type student growing up. When I went to college at LSU, I failed a speech class. I was so terrified of speaking in front of the other students (only about thirty) in my class that I could barely get through my presentation. Who knew that God would eventually have me speak in front of tens of thousands of people every weekend?

I sure didn't. And I was in danger of living the unredeemed life. The only way I even started living as God intended is that God used other people to see the potential in me that I never would have seen in myself. Some of these people prophesied to me about my future. Others encouraged, challenged, and enhanced my abilities. I'm convinced that it often takes others to see our God-given potential, because we tend to limit ourselves by becoming too self-critical.

* * *

The other way God promises to redeem us is through "mighty acts of judgment." Now before you start thinking that this sounds contradictory to pulling us up and pushing us toward our greatness, you need to realize what—and whom—God is judging with his mighty acts. God's mighty acts of judgment are reserved for the enemy of our souls. Like any protective parent, God never hesitates to confront his kids' enemy.

You see, the devil has his own plan for your life. He'll do anything to obscure your identity as a child of God and derail your true purpose. Your enemy wants you to think so lowly of yourself that you won't even attempt what God has created you to do. The devil's going to undermine your efforts and try to keep you from finding your dream. And he'll put anything he can in your way.

Even someone as accomplished as the apostle Paul experienced this resistance many times. In 1 Thessalonians 2:18, he writes, "We wanted very much to come to you, and I, Paul, tried again and again, but Satan prevented us." The Greek for "prevented" is *egkoptō*, which means to cut a ditch across the road. It's what robbers would do to force travelers to stop so that they were sitting ducks. This "ditch" impedes our progress by cutting off our path and creating a diversion so we'll take a different route.

Satan loves to use our everyday problems to create diversions in our lives. He doesn't want us drinking from the Cup of Redemption. To hinder us and prevent us from traveling down God's redemptive road, the enemy will try to make us spiritually nearsighted. He doesn't want us to see the big picture—the timeless plan that God has for us. Instead, the devil wants to keep us focused on our-selves, our issues, our own comfort and convenience. But God keeps reaching down and pulling us up. That's why the apostle Paul writes, "We are pressed on every side by troubles, but we are not crushed. We are perplexed, but not driven to despair. We are hunted down, but never abandoned by God. We get knocked down, but we are not destroyed (2 Corinthians 4:8-9).

> The devil wants to keep us focused on ourselves, our issues, our own comfort and convenience. But God keeps reaching down and pulling us up.

How is it that Paul faced all kinds of problems and yet he was never derailed from his calling? He learned the secret of *focus*. "Our present troubles are small and won't last very long. Yet they produce for us a glory that vastly outweighs them and will last forever! So we don't look at the troubles we can see now; rather, we fix our gaze on things that cannot be seen. For the things we see now will soon be gone, but the things we cannot see will last forever" (2 Corinthians 4:17-18).

The truth is, it's easy to become nearsighted, focusing only on our own everyday problems. You can always tell if someone is spiritually nearsighted by their prayers. Do they pray big prayers that will change the world? Or do they pray about what they want in their immediate cir-cumstances? If the devil can't keep you out of heaven, then he'd at least like you to be ineffective in the meantime.

He'd love for you never to make it beyond the second cup, always struggling on the treadmill of deliverance from your own self-absorption.

Instead, we must experience and practice the deliverance promised in the second cup and then drink deeply from the third cup—the Cup of Redemption. God wants us to grow, discover, and develop into the realization of our full potential. Otherwise, we'll remain nearsighted and unproductive, and that falls right into the plan of the enemy.

> *For this very reason, make every effort to add to your faith goodness; and to goodness, knowledge; and to knowledge, self-control; and to self-control, perseverance; and to perseverance, godliness; and to godliness, brotherly kindness; and to brotherly kindness, love. For if you possess these qualities in increasing measure, they will keep you from being ineffective and unproductive in your knowledge of our Lord Jesus Christ. But if anyone does not have them, he is nearsighted and blind, and has forgotten that he has been cleansed from his past sins.*
>
> 2 PETER 1:5-9, NIV

✳ ✳ ✳

So how do you find your redemptive calling? The best way to discover your divine destiny (what God wants you to do) is to understand your divine design (how God made you). To put it simply, your design will reveal your destiny.

Let me explain. Because you are "God's workmanship, created in Christ Jesus to do good works, which God prepared in advance for us to do" (Ephesians 2:10, NIV), you can trust that God deliberately made you the way you are. He didn't create you and then think, *Hmm, now what can I do with this one?* God did not breathe life into you and then decide what your purpose would be. Just the opposite. God had something in mind for you to do and then he created you to do it. He saw a need, a hole, a vacancy in the world, and designed you in order to fill it.

The first step in finding your purpose is to get free from bondage. This occurs as you drink from the first cup of God's promise to you—he *saves* you. The next step requires letting God heal the pain and scars of yesterday; this is the second cup, *deliverance.* Too many people rush through the second cup or ignore it altogether and want to race onward to their purpose. But we can never live out our purpose until we've dealt with our past wounds.

We see this clearly in the parable of the talents in Matthew 25. The three servants were not all given the same number of talents: one received five, the next got two, and the third got only one. But they all had the same opportunity to use their talents wisely and profitably on behalf of their master. The only difference was that the servant with only one talent allowed his fear to produce failure. He saw his master as a hard, unreasonable, overbearing judge instead of as a kind father.

If you live by fear, you will bury your talent. Instead,

you must bury your fear and invest your talent. Once your fears, pains, and limitations are confessed and healed, it's time to explore your personality, gifts, passions, and dreams. Within the treasure chest of your divine design, you will discover your destiny.

It all begins by discovering who God made you to be. Once you begin living out of what you discover, then the fun really starts. From the four basic Greek temperaments to the Myers-Briggs personality types, there are many different ways to explore the way you were designed by God. Take a minute to thank God for how he designed you: "You made all the delicate, inner parts of my body and knit me together in my mother's womb. Thank you for making me so wonderfully complex! Your workmanship is marvelous—how well I know it" (Psalm 139:13-14).

✳ ✳ ✳

Another primary area of self-discovery involves spiritual gifts. When we become Christians and the Holy Spirit indwells us, he brings a spiritual gifting that works in harmony with our personality, experiences, and abilities. A spiritual gift is a special, supernatural ability that God gives to each of his children so that together we can advance his purposes in the world.

We each have different spiritual gifts that God has placed in us to fulfill our purpose and advance his Kingdom. As Paul explains, "There are *different* kinds of spiritual gifts, but the *same* Spirit is the source of them all. There are *different* kinds of service, but we serve the *same* Lord. God works in *different* ways, but it is the *same* God who does the work in all of us. A spiritual gift is given to each of us so we can help each other" (1 Corinthians 12:4-7, emphasis added). Notice that in this passage, the words *different* and *same* are used three times. God wants to emphasize that each of us is unique and different from everyone else, but that we're all united in serving the same God.

Even in the exact same situation, people with different spiritual gifts will view the situation differently. My friend and fellow pastor Rick Warren has a great way of illustrating these differences. He says to imagine that each spiritual gift is represented as a family member at the dinner table. If someone dropped their dessert on the floor, here's how each family member (spiritual gift) would respond:

> **Mercy:** "Don't feel bad, it could have happened to anybody."
> **Preaching:** "That's what happens when you're not careful!"
> **Serving:** "Let me help you clean it up."
> **Teaching:** "The reason it fell is because it was too heavy on one side."
> **Exhortation:** "Next time, let's serve the dessert with the meal."
> **Giving:** "I'll be happy to buy you a new dessert."

Administration: "Jim, would you get the mop?
Sue, pick it up. Mary, help me fix another
dessert."[2]

There are certainly more spiritual gifts than these, but
you get the point. We each naturally focus on different
areas of service that come naturally to us. Every gift is
good because it comes from God (James 1:17). One is
not better than another. Our different personality traits,
temperaments, or spiritual gifts are not to be measured or
compared with one another, as if some have more worth or
value than others. There is no room for inferiority or envy
in the body of Christ; we are all "fearfully and wonderfully
made" (Psalm 139:14, NIV).

Whatever your personality type, you are still to bear the
fruit of the Spirit in your life. Personality types and spiritual gifts don't give us an excuse to be unloving, unkind,
unfairly critical, or judgmental. Although you cannot
change your personality or spiritual gifts, you can redeem
them through the power of the Holy Spirit, who is the one
source of them all (1 Corinthians 12:4).

When you struggle with knowing your purpose or feel
challenged in pursuing it, keep in mind how the redemptive power of God redeemed the nation of Israel. God took
them from slaves in the mud pits of Egypt to become some
of the most influential and successful people in the world.

Some of the greatest minds in human history have
been Jewish. To date, Jewish people have won more than

20 percent of the total number of Nobel Prizes awarded (187 of 800), even though the Jews comprise less than two-tenths of one percent of the world's population. I would say that God has indeed redeemed them with an outstretched arm and with mighty acts of judgment!

The same God who redeemed and restored the Jewish people has equipped each follower of Jesus with the gifts and attributes needed to fulfill his purpose. But as I have worked with members of our church and spoken to pastors of other churches, I've found that more than 80 percent of the people in our churches have never discovered what makes them unique—they've never discovered their redemptive calling. The Bible says that every one of us is a part of the body of Christ and every one of us has a different and important function (1 Corinthians 12:27). Can

> *The same God who redeemed and restored the Jewish people has equipped each follower of Jesus with the gifts and attributes needed to fulfill his purpose.*

you imagine what your body would be like if 80 percent of it didn't know what it was or how to function? You would probably be dead, or an invalid at the very least. When we discover and develop our redemptive calling, we not only live lives of purpose and fulfillment, but we also become a complete body, one that God can use in mighty ways.

God is omnipotent—all potential is in him. And God's potential is great in you. The closer you draw to him, the more he will reveal to you the plan he's had for you since before you were even born. Let God take you on a journey of incredible redemption. Drink from the third cup of promise. Here's a simple prayer to get you started:

> *Father, thank you for designing a purpose for me before time began. Thank you for the gifts you have given me so I can serve you. Open the eyes of my heart and let me see myself the way you see me. Give me wisdom to discover, develop, and live out the redemptive plan you have for my life. I give my life—and all my talents, gifts, and abilities—to you. Amen.*

CHAPTER SEVEN

THE CUP OF PRAISE

I will take you as my own people,

and I will be your God.

EXODUS 6:7, NIV

HALLELUJAH is a funny word that many Christians use to rejoice, even if they don't quite know what it means. But they're right on target. The root word, *hallel*, means to celebrate, boast, or rave—an exclamation of victory after one has experienced some level of fulfillment.

It's understandable, then, that the Jewish people call the last cup of the Passover Seder hallel, because with it they celebrate the fact that they were formed into a new nation after their rescue and deliverance from Egypt. They rejoice in their identity as part of God's family. And they praise God for giving them a fulfilled life, a purposeful life that makes a difference in the world.

When we live out our dreams (fulfillment), praise just naturally occurs. That's why I sometimes refer to this final cup as the Cup of Fulfillment. It's all about being a part of God's Kingdom, being his son or his daughter, and having a family to belong to. It's about knowing that you're part of something bigger than yourself and working alongside others to fulfill God's plan.

No one reminds me that I'm part of something bigger more than Tommy Barnett, one of my heroes in ministry. Pastor of Phoenix First Assembly of God, he's also a cofounder, with his son Matthew, of the Los Angeles Dream Center, a volunteer-based ministry that facilitates multiple facets of healing for individuals and families in need. Pastor Barnett is well into his seventies and still pursuing big things for God with more passion and energy than men half his age.

In a recent interview, he was asked, "Now that you're

over seventy, do you have any regrets? Anything you wish you'd done differently in your life?" Without hesitating, Tommy said, "Yes—two. I wish I would've dreamed bigger. And I wish I would've risked more."[3] Coming from a person who, from my perspective, has done more to advance God's Kingdom than most people I know, his response shocked me. But somewhere in his response is the attitude that epitomizes our fourth cup of promise, the Cup of Praise.

* * *

We often talk about "living the dream" to refer to someone who's really successful and doing what they love. Or we use it to mean the exact opposite—a sarcastic response when someone who feels stuck is asked how they're doing. But God intends for us to literally live our dreams—the dreams he's placed inside of us. This is the only way we can come to know a contentment, a joy, and a sense of wholeness that money can't buy and material comforts can't touch.

God's ultimate plan for you is to be full *and* filled— fulfilled. He wants you living life to the fullest. The enemy of our souls, on the other hand, is committed to robbing us of joy, meaning, and purpose. Jesus makes this contrast very clear: "The thief's purpose is to steal, kill, and destroy. My purpose is to give life in all its fullness" (John 10:10, TLB).

> God's ultimate plan for you is to be full and filled—fulfilled. He wants you living life to the fullest.

From what I've witnessed, most people don't reach this fourth cup. They get caught somewhere along the journey and become stuck in one place. Why? Because, even if they discover their calling, or at least some sense of what it is, they don't live it out. I'm convinced that fear-based procrastination keeps people from living to the fullest.

The ultimate purpose of the four cups of promise is for us to live the unlived life within us. Brian Houston, senior pastor of Hillsong Church in Australia, epitomizes the fourth cup as he challenges Christians to live their unlived lives. In one of his messages, he urged everyone:

Pursue that project that you've been dreaming about
Start that diet and health routine
Finish that degree
Learn how to play that instrument
Finally address that addiction or unhealthy habit
Commit to your local church and get involved
Write that book
Compose that song

It's not that you need to do all these things or feel pressured to be a perfect person. It's simply that God placed dreams and divine desires in you for a reason. He didn't give you that dream so that you could constantly feel frustrated and defeated. You may not be able to imagine how your dream could come about—and maybe that's how it should be because that means you'll have to rely on God as your power source. When you bury your talents because you're afraid, lazy, or too shortsighted to invest them in your God-given dream, then your life becomes a tragedy of eternal regret.

* * *

So how do you drink from this fourth cup and move forward toward the dreams God has for you? Though it varies with each individual, I'll share some of the ways I do it. Almost weekly, I review my bucket list—you know, the things I want to do before I "kick the bucket." My list includes three major categories: (1) *relational pursuits*: things I want to do and places I want to go with my family; (2) *ministry pursuits*: dreams I have for serving God and equipping others; and (3) *thrills*: a random assortment of things I want to see, do, and experience. With more than a hundred items on my list, I suspect that half may never get checked off. But I also know that if I don't have a target, I'll hit it every time.

I encourage you to write out your own version. Include not only the things that are certain or likely to happen, but make sure to list at least a few that are completely ridiculous, crazy, and seemingly impossible.

My bucket list reminds me that living out my dreams is the secret to happiness. And I know that real happiness doesn't come from climbing mountains or writing bestsellers. The happiest people on the planet are those who are making a difference in the lives of other people—because that's how God designed us.

He put a deep desire inside of every person's heart, a desire that's not only important to God, but that also meets our greatest need when it's fulfilled. King Solomon said it best: "He has made everything beautiful in its time. He also has planted eternity in men's hearts and minds [a divinely implanted sense of a purpose working through the ages which nothing under the sun but God alone can satisfy], yet so that men cannot find out what God has done from the beginning to the end" (Ecclesiastes 3:11, AMP).

> *God put a deep desire inside of every person's heart, a desire that's not only important to God, but that also meets our greatest need when it's fulfilled.*

As you consider your deepest needs, it may be helpful to reference American psychologist Abraham Maslow's "hierarchy of needs," a theory of human motivation based on five levels of human need: physiological, safety, love, esteem, and self-actualization. Maslow believed that people are motivated by their pursuit of solutions to these needs—beginning with our basic physical needs and moving upward through the other stages as each successive level of need is met. As we achieve and become secure at each level of need, we become aware of the next level of need and take action to attain it.

I'm convinced that Maslow was right, and that his theory, which has been widely popularized for more than seventy years, reveals how God designed us. Maslow believed that we seek fulfillment—from our most basic needs to everything we are capable of becoming—not only to survive, but also to give our lives meaning.

Maslow's original article focused on five needs, but as others have studied and applied his theory, the list has expanded to eight, including needs that reflect our highest aspirations for personal fulfillment. As you briefly consider each one, think about how much of your time, energy, and resources you currently spend in pursuing these needs. The first four needs—called "deficiency" needs—are things you need in order to live and avoid negative consequences. These are ongoing needs that must be continually satisfied, or you will experience deprivation or deficiency. The deficiency needs include:

1. Physical needs. These are biological and physiological needs such as air, food, water, shelter, warmth, and sleep. Studies show that 85 percent of people in the United States have these basic needs met.

2. Safety needs. We need protection from the elements as well as security, order, law, limits, and stability. It's why we lock doors, learn self-defense, carry weapons, and stay with what's familiar even if it's not good for us (such as a bad job or relationship). Research indicates that about 75 percent of people in our country have these needs met.

3. Love needs. Everyone longs to be loved and belong. We need family, affection, and healthy relationships.

This is why social media are so popular—we all want to be connected to others in meaningful ways. About 50 percent of people say they have these needs met.

4. Esteem needs. These include self-esteem, achievement, recognition, and the desire to be appreciated and valued. This usually comes down to what we think about ourselves, what others think about us, and what we think others think about us (our appearance, clothes, house, car, job, etc.). Of people surveyed, roughly 40 percent indicate these needs are met satisfactorily.

The final four are higher order needs, or "growth" needs— things that contribute to our growth and fulfillment. These needs are more abstract and long-term, but they represent what brings true fulfillment and makes us truly happy. All of these needs, except for self-actualization, were added to the list after Maslow's original grouping.

5. Cognitive needs. We all need mental stimulation: knowledge, meaning, solutions, and analysis. We want and need to understand how certain things work and change. It's why we enjoy watching *Planet Earth* on Discovery Channel or why some people devote their lives to the study of certain works or topics.

6. Aesthetic needs. People have an innate appreciation for order and beauty and desire it as a consistent

part of their lives. It may be reflected in a love of nature and the outdoors or a passion for mountains, beaches, animals, or weather. These needs reflect why we prefer one style of home over another, or why we like to sing, draw, paint, write, or design clothes. It's why we want certain pictures on the walls that are painted particular colors.

7. Self-actualization needs. This is a basic need to realize our personal potential, a sense of being the best self we were created to be. It's reflected in our pursuit of goals with unwavering excellence, regardless of our field of endeavor. It could be seeking peak experiences on the football field or in the research lab, or becoming an expert because of a passion and understanding of our deepest desires. God put a desire in each of us to reach this potential, and yet studies show that only 2 percent of people in America live at this level of fulfillment. An interesting side note: only 0.1 percent of college students have a sense of fulfillment in their lives.

8. Transcendence needs. Maslow assumed self-actualization was the highest need, but this one is even higher. It's the greatest need in a person's life, the ultimate motivator that explains why we get up in the morning and endure all that life throws at us. It's reflected in compassion, sympathy, and caregiving; times when we look beyond our own

needs and help others, not out of obligation but from the joy of helping to meet someone else's needs. This need can only be met when our other needs have been satisfied. We can't help someone else if our own needs are unmet. Transcendent living is what the fourth cup is all about.[4]

✳ ✳ ✳

I love the word *transcendent*. My handy *Webster's* dictionary defines it as "exceeding usual limits, surpassing," and "extending beyond the limits of ordinary experience, beyond comprehension." This definition reminds me of a verse in Ephesians: "Now glory be to God, who by his mighty power at work within us is able to do far more than we would ever dare to ask or even dream of—infinitely beyond our highest prayers, desires, thoughts, or hopes" (Ephesians 3:20, TLB). Ultimately, the fourth cup is about doing something beyond ourselves, living life beyond limits. This is only possible when we're serving an extraordinary God.

Most people don't see themselves as world changers. But that's how God sees us. We all want satisfaction in life, but the satisfaction most people are looking for comes from being in the middle of the action, not on the sidelines. Our lives will radically change when we find our best fit, get equipped, and serve others. Ultimate fulfillment comes when we live beyond ourselves and pour our passion into service; when we do that, we change the world.

I saw this in action firsthand when I was a youth pastor

in Colorado. I led a summer camp each year that helped transform hundreds of teenagers into world changers. Our leadership team was convinced that if these young men and women had a global worldview, if they understood that God wanted to use them in his grand design for great things, then the trivial issues that plague most teens would fall away.

The fourth cup is about doing something beyond ourselves, living life beyond limits.

It worked. After eleven years of youth ministry, I had witnessed some amazing transformations. Very few students got caught up in the drug scene, the party scene, or even the dating scene. Instead, most went on mission trips, volunteered in various ministries, or found some unique way to serve others with their gifts. The secret is that they saw themselves as world changers.

So why don't we all see ourselves this way?

Historically, people have assumed there are two kinds of Christians: ministers and non-ministers. This model seems to find its roots in the Old Testament, where it's explicitly clear that God's Spirit worked through priests and high priests, special people with supernatural assignments from God.

But in the New Testament, everything changes when Jesus arrives on the scene. He looks at ordinary people and says, "You are the light of the world. . . . You will receive power when the Holy Spirit comes upon you. And

you will be my witnesses . . . to the ends of the earth"
(Matthew 5:14; Acts 1:8). The message is clear: God wants
his power in every person's life. He loves taking ordinary
people and using them to do extraordinary things.

It didn't take long, however, for Christians to make ministry a profession and hire a few folks to lead their churches. They called these people *clergy* and soon the rest of the body of Christ

> *God wants his power in every person's life. He loves taking ordinary people and using them to do extraordinary things.*

sat passively on the sidelines and watched. They could be
part of a "church" without any real sacrifice or personal
commitment to the well-being of the community.

The Protestant Reformation in the 1500s tried to shake
things up. It emphasized the "new" revelation that we were
all part of the "priesthood of believers." But nothing really
changed. There were still two groups: clergy and laity.
Unfortunately, that's still the way the vast majority see
it today. And that's why many Christians struggle, wondering why they're so unfulfilled. And churches struggle
without all parts of the body of Christ participating.

✳ ✳ ✳

When I started Church of the Highlands in Birmingham,
I often went out to eat with our new members. One day I
was lunching with a guy named Bill Borland, who went by
"Buzz." While we were eating and getting acquainted, Buzz

saw a friend across the restaurant and motioned him over. When his friend approached our table, Buzz introduced me as his "preacher" (add a thick Southern accent), and we all chatted before his friend returned to his own table. Once Buzz and I sat back down, I said, "I'm not your preacher!"

"Sure you are!" Buzz replied good-naturedly. It was clear in his mind that preachers were supposed to come up with a good sermon each week, and visit hospitals and the unsaved in between Sundays.

"No," I said emphatically, "*you're* the preacher! My job is to *equip* you to do ministry."

My lunch with Buzz was an eye-opener. I realized most Christians really had no clue about a pastor's true role. In Ephesians 4:11-12, God provides pastors (as well as apostles, prophets, evangelists, and shepherds) "to equip God's people to do his work and build up the church, the body of Christ" (v. 12). There's not one ounce of biblical support for the traditional clergy/laity split. It's clearly not what God had in mind.

Instead, a ton of evidence in Scripture indicates that God wants *all* of his children to serve as his ambassadors. The Bible is clear that every Christian is called by God to change the world. "You are a chosen people, a royal priesthood, a holy nation, a people belonging to God, that you may declare the praises of him who called you out of darkness into his wonderful light" (1 Peter 2:9, NIV).

We're all ministers and we're all called to serve. People want to think that, because I'm a pastor, I have a better connection to God. But I don't. When I'm playing golf and bad weather threatens, someone usually says, "You're a preacher—do something!" I smile and say, "I'm in sales, not management."

Even though our gifts and contributions may differ, we're all equally important. Just because my gift is leadership does not make me better or more important. "God has given each of you a gift from his great variety of spiritual gifts. Use them well to serve one another" (1 Peter 4:10).

We're all vitally and equally important, because we're all uniquely created by God for different purposes. He deliberately wired us differently. You're not one in a million—you're one of a kind! Some people think of themselves as average, with next to nothing to contribute. And it doesn't help that the devil reinforces this notion by whispering, "You don't matter. You're nothing special. You aren't important here."

But this is not true. The Bible is very clear about this: "God's various gifts are handed out everywhere; but they all originate in God's Spirit. God's various ministries are carried out everywhere; but they all originate in God's Spirit. God's various expressions of power are in action everywhere; but God himself is behind it all. Each person is given something to do that shows who God is: Everyone gets in on it, everyone benefits. All kinds of things are handed out by the Spirit, and to all kinds of people! The variety is wonderful" (1 Corinthians 12:4-7, MSG). We all need to embrace our uniqueness and our giftedness.

When we embrace the fact that we are unique and special, we can begin to experience true fulfillment. My greatest passion is for people to find and live out their God-given passion. There's no better feeling than when we're serving God in whatever capacity he's created for us to serve. The ultimate goal is for us to be able to say, "I was made for this!"

Unfortunately, some people—and you may be one of them—go around thinking, *It's too late. I've already messed up my life. The mess is too big and too complicated to unravel.* Don't believe it! God can even take our failures and turn them into a gift he can use. Tell me,

> True fulfillment never comes alone; it can only be attained within a group of people.

who better to sit down with someone struggling through a divorce than someone who's been there? Who better to help out parents struggling with their kids than parents who have already been through those same kinds of struggles?

Ultimate fulfillment is about ministering to others from our own unique stories.

✳ ✳ ✳

Ultimate fulfillment also comes from being part of a team. Notice how God worded his final promise in Exodus 6:7: "I will claim you as my own people." He never promised to make you a fulfilled *person*, in isolation. He promised to make you *part of the family*, his own people. True fulfillment never comes alone; it can only be attained within a group of people.

I'm convinced that people are ultimately looking for three things. And all three can only happen when we're part of a team. I call them the Three Cs of teamwork.

First, everyone wants to make a *contribution*. We all want *progress*, not just perspective and participation. We all want to help make things happen, and we always make better progress in a group.

Next, everyone wants *community*. One of the greatest joys of teamwork is being on the team. It's how God made us—as communal beings, not as detached islands. This is why the enemy of our souls goes to great lengths to try to destroy our relationships. He's trying to stop our potential to make a difference.

> *When we invest in each other's lives and work to accomplish God's goals together, it's so much more enjoyable to celebrate together.*

Finally, everyone wants a *celebration*. Parties are fun, but not when we're alone. Sports are fun, but not when we're alone. When we invest in each other's lives and work to accomplish God's goals together, it's so much more enjoyable to celebrate together. We all share in the victory and have an increased awareness of God's goodness.

Whether or not we're aware of it, we are needed. God designed us to be a vitally important part of his plan. Other people are waiting on us right now to join them in making a difference. It's time to drink from the fourth cup.

Here is a simple prayer to start drinking from the Cup of Praise:

> *Father, thank you for designing me to live life to the full. Thank you for making me part of your family with so many remarkable brothers and sisters. I'm amazed at all you've given me and at all that you call me to do for your Kingdom. I praise you, Lord, and give you thanks for your goodness, kindness, and mercy. Thank you for your four cups of promise and the privilege of drinking from each one. Amen.*

A MODEL FOR CHURCH LEADERS

The churches were strengthened in their

faith and grew larger every day.

ACTS 16:5

SINCE THE BEGINNING of Church of the Highlands in 2001, we've dedicated the first twenty-one days of each new year to prayer and fasting. One of the things we do during this season is have morning prayer at the church campuses from 6:00 to 7:00 a.m. People can worship together, pray on their own for thirty minutes, and then join together for corporate prayer.

Several years ago, while attending one of these prayer meetings, I heard God speak to me. When I say that, I don't mean I actually heard an audible voice. But I'm not talking about an "impression" either. I have many of those daily that I often think are from God. This one was different. It was clear and it came with a sense of responsibility—I call it a burden. When I say it was different, it was a moment that I haven't had but two other times: the night God called me to vocational ministry at the age of twenty, and the day God called me to Birmingham in May 2000.

This time I heard God say, *Help a thousand churches under a thousand in attendance grow and reach their full potential.* I began to pray about this vision and ideas immediately came to mind of how we could do something like that. I put a team of my staff together and began dreaming with them about how we could train, resource, and come alongside other pastors and churches to help them reach their full potential.

I didn't want to be presumptuous and assume that pastors actually wanted our help, so we decided to pilot the idea and offer a two-day training for pastors who wanted some help growing their churches. We didn't advertise it at all—I simply put it out on Twitter. More than four hundred pastors registered to come to the first training, which we called the GROW Leadership Intensive. Now, three years later, we assist more than two thousand pastors annually through training, resourcing, and coaching. It's one of the most fulfilling things I do. In fact, I *know* I was made for this.

✳ ✳ ✳

I doubt you'll be surprised when I tell you that the Four Cups have become my filter for ministry and what we teach other churches. At our church, we focus on four areas because I'm convinced that it has always been in God's heart to do these four things in our lives. In fact, I believe this is God's vision for every person and every church.

For me, the question isn't *what* to do—it's *how* to do it. And please understand that there isn't just one way. Systems are what we do to accomplish a vision; it's our programming, our track to run on. I fully support other people having different systems. And I'm fine with their having strong opinions about their systems. I share the way we live out the Four Cups at Church of the Highlands as *inspiration* and *encouragement*, not as an exclusive model.

I'm not in love with our model. I'm committed to seeing people saved, delivered, redeemed, and fulfilled. Here's how we define success at our church: *when people are moving from where they are to where God wants them to be.* Our definition is the essence of the Four Cups of Promise. We want to see the lost saved, the saved delivered from their issues, the delivered discovering their redemptive calling, and those who have discovered their redemptive calling living it out by being part of a team that is making a difference. Regardless of how you do it at your church, if you're willing to use God's promises in the Four Cups to guide you, then without a doubt you will take people on an amazing journey of growth. Here are the ways that we have applied the Four Cups in our church.

1. THE CUP OF SALVATION: WEEKEND SERVICES

Setting people free from the bondage of sin by sharing the good news of Jesus Christ is our highest priority and our most important step. The other three cups build on this first one. And truthfully, the first cup is the only one that is needed for eternal life. So nothing is closer to the heart of God than saving his people. We see this in Luke 15 and its parables of the lost sheep, the lost coin, and the lost son. Clearly, finding his lost children is God's priority. In every story, the message is clear: God is more focused on the lost than he is on the found. It's why he sent his only Son to die for us.

Several years ago, while our family was on vacation, Joseph, the youngest of our five children, just disappeared. He was only eleven years old at the time, and he is on the autism spectrum and has difficulty communicating with other people. We were with several families, going from store to store, shopping and eating, and Joseph had decided to find a bathroom without telling us. When he came out of the bathroom, we had already moved farther down the street, and he decided to go the other direction to find us. It wasn't long before we realized he was missing, and we were in a panic. Frantically, the whole family dispersed in different directions looking for Joseph. For thirty-five minutes (which seemed like eternity) he was gone.

When I approached a security guard, he seemed disinterested and certainly didn't have the sense of urgency I had to find my son. With his hands in his pockets, he said, "Well, have you looked the last place you saw him?" His response irritated me, and I said, "You're the one with the radio! Help me find him!" I was so frustrated by his passivity and inactivity.

Sometimes I imagine that God feels very much the same way. He just wants us to help him find his lost kids. There was never a moment in the search when I thought, *I have four other kids. Eighty percent isn't bad.* No, in fact I never even thought about my other kids at that moment. I just wanted to find Joseph. My kids were all helping in the search, but had any of them come to me during that time and said, "Dad, how about an ice cream?" I would have thought, *You really don't get it, do you?*

Again, I imagine God feels the same way when we ask him for things for ourselves when he's concerned about his lost kids. Yes, he enjoys answering our prayers and giving us good things. But nothing means more to him than finding the kids who are still lost.

When we found Joseph, we felt so grateful and relieved, but that's still only a fraction of what God must feel when a lost son or daughter comes home to him. Jesus made a promise that if we'd focus on reaching the lost, he would be with us, even to the end of the age. So we made a decision to make the Cup of Salvation a priority at our church.

We have discovered that it's easiest to share the Cup of Salvation in our Sunday services. Our goal is to create an environment in which people can get saved. We have to continually remind ourselves that the church doesn't exist only for those already there, but for those who are not there yet. There's a natural, gravitational pull to create experiences for those of us already in the family of God—and certainly this is important and has its place. (More on this in a moment.)

But if we want to do ministry like Jesus, then we need sinners around us. As holy as he was, he attracted people from every walk of life. The sinners and outcasts of his day—prostitutes, tax collectors, adulterers, lepers—enjoyed being in his presence. They never felt inferior or looked down upon or condemned by Jesus. We can't let our churches become an environment where the lost don't come or want to visit.

God is more concerned about the outsider than the insider. He is more concerned about the lost than the found. The question is *how* to naturally appeal to the lost. How can evangelism be hassle-free and remain powerful?

How can it be appealing and natural without becoming goofy or overly sentimental? Some Christians are concerned that we're being too soft and watering down the gospel. And don't get me wrong—there's a place to be confrontational. But it's later in the journey. We would do well to remember that "God's kindness leads you toward repentance" (Romans 2:4, NIV).

We must go their way to reach them. Paul, the apostle to the Gentiles (non-Jewish people), wrote, "I have made myself a slave to everyone, to win as many as possible. . . . I have become all things to all men so that by all possible means I might save some" (1 Corinthians 9:19, 22, NIV).

So we constantly ask ourselves, "Are we attracting the lost? Are they coming? Are the ones who are coming experiencing the first cup? Are people getting saved?" If we can't answer yes to every one of these questions, then we make some changes. We ask for feedback. We try to be as constructively critical as possible so that we can create a place where people long to quench their thirst for the Living God by drinking of his first cup—the Living Water of salvation through his Son, Jesus Christ.

2. THE CUP OF DELIVERANCE: DYNAMIC SMALL GROUPS

After they got out of Egypt, the children of Israel were no longer slaves, but they still had the mind-set and attitudes of slaves. They did not know how to be liberated people in relationship with their loving Father. They were saved from the bondage of Egypt, but their old ways were still ruling their lives. For us, we find freedom from sin when we get saved, but usually we're still allowing sin to rule our lives.

As you'll recall from our discussion of the second cup, salvation is instant, but deliverance is a process. "My dear friends, . . . continue to work out your salvation with fear and trembling, for it is God who works in you to will and to act according to his good purpose" (Philippians 2:12-13, NIV). Once again, most of us can agree that we need to work out our faith with fear and trembling, but how do we go about it? How do we deal with our personal issues and most shameful secrets? In a public group, with mostly strangers? Or in the safety of people we've come to know and trust?

Some people say, "I'll work it out with God privately—it's just between him and me." The only problem is that that's not God's plan. His Word could not be any clearer: We go to God for forgiveness (1 John 1:9) and we go to God's people for healing (James 5:16). Small groups are where we deal with our ugly stuff and live out our faith as a process. As we live our lives together with other followers of Jesus, we earn the right to speak and be heard—to be honest and transparent with one another. We create a safe place where we know we're loved and valued, no matter how ugly our struggles or how painful our admissions.

Real life change happens in the context of relationships. Always has, always will. Information alone has never changed anyone's life. God uses *people*. And that's why we need to follow God's formula to experience real deliverance.

> *Let us hold tightly without wavering to the hope we affirm, for God can be trusted to keep his promise. Let us think of ways to motivate one another to acts of love and good works. And let us not neglect our meeting together, as some people do, but encourage one another, especially now that the day of his return is drawing near.*
>
> HEBREWS 10:23-25

That's why we encourage everyone at our church to be in a weekly small group with other believers. Small groups are not mini church services; and they're not necessarily even Bible studies (though most groups study some type of Bible-based curriculum). They are intimate gatherings where relationships form and an environment is created where there can be real transparency. In my previous book, *Fresh Air*, I write about the power of spiritual community and how we all want to go where everybody knows our name.

Everyone needs to be a known and valued member of a small group. If our Sunday services are to offer the Cup of Salvation, then our small groups offer ongoing tastes of the Cup of Deliverance. In order to keep people growing and living in the freedom God promises us, we frequently ask ourselves, "Are those who are in our church experiencing the second cup? Are people working through their issues? Are people getting close to other believers and experiencing healing?"

3. THE CUP OF REDEMPTION: AN INTENTIONAL GROWTH-TRACK PROCESS

This is part of the Christian journey that a lot of believers never get to experience. If they get bogged down in the Cup of Deliverance, they may not grow into the fullness of freedom that allows them to discover their purpose and live it out. But that's actually our main job! It's why we were created. When we discover what we're made for, we experience a level of contentment and joy that's without equal.

As we practice our gifts and serve others, we equip others so that they can live freely and use their own unique gifts and abilities. This is the purpose of pastors and church leaders—to equip each of the saints.

> To each one of us grace has been given as Christ
> apportioned it. . . . It was he who gave some to be
> apostles, some to be prophets, some to be evangelists,
> and some to be pastors and teachers, to prepare God's
> people for works of service, so that the body of Christ
> may be built up until we all reach unity in the faith
> and in the knowledge of the Son of God and become
> mature, attaining to the whole measure of the fullness
> of Christ.
>
> EPHESIANS 4:7, 11-13, NIV

We're supposed to help people find and develop their grace gifts. The Greek word for "grace" is *charis*, from which we get our word for charity—giving to others from the abundance we have received. Every believer has a divine enablement, and yet many don't know what it is. It's not just a matter of giving people more information and training, as if they're robots that can be programmed. Instead, it's a *relationship*. The entire discipleship process begins by helping other people discover the gifts inside them. Then we help them develop those gifts to be used for God's glory.

In many cases, Christians think that *discipleship* means just learning more about God and the Bible. Learning is important, but directed learning is better. For example, you wouldn't go to college and just take classes. You begin the whole process of getting a degree by declaring a major or having in mind a job you'd like to do when you get done with school. In the same way, you'll be a better disciple of Christ if you discover your calling and *then* take the classes.

No matter what our unique gifting might be, our job is to help every believer discover why they were created. At Church of the Highlands, we've found that we need a clearly defined track to get them there. This is where church can get really fun!

Every month, we offer a set of four classes to help people drink from the Cup of Redemption. First, they need a relationship with a local church. We call it Church 101— it's our membership class. By God's design, people need to commit to a community of believers and get connected to the other members of that community. The first step is to find a life-giving church.

Second, they need to be taught how to have a vibrant relationship with God. So the second step in the Highlands growth track is Essentials 201. Why? Because in order for us to discover our redemptive calling, we need to connect to the only one who has the book on our lives (Psalm 139). The closer we are to God, the more we discover what he has in store for our lives.

The third step is a systematic discovery process we call Discovery 301. By using a simple personality assessment and spiritual gifts assessment, people can find their destiny by understanding their design.

Ultimately, the real secret of discovering our redemptive calling can only come through trial and error. So we take people through their first service opportunity with a class called Dream Team 401. This class gives people the opportunity to experiment with different types of functions and places of service to really know if that's what God wants them to do. One of the best things we do is allow people to try different areas of ministry within the church before they make a long-term commitment to that area. Most of the growth in our personal discipleship will happen *after* we start doing something with our lives—not before. That's when real discipleship happens: just doing it.

So we ask ourselves regularly, "Are people experiencing the third cup? Are they discovering their redemptive calling? Are they being developed to change the world?" We want to make sure that everything we do contributes to equipping and unleashing world changers.

4. THE CUP OF PRAISE: THE DREAM TEAM

From the early days, even before we launched our church, I put together a group of people that I originally called the Launch Team. But I was having trouble getting the team to help me come up with ideas about our new church. They had all been conditioned to just be told what to do—much of which came from previous church experiences where the leaders were the only ones who had rights to the vision.

Because I wanted them to *dream* with me, I decided one night at a team meeting, about two months before our launch, to rename them the Dream Team. Not only because I saw them as the ultimate team (like the US men's basketball team—the first to feature active NBA players— that dominated in the 1992 Olympics), but also because I really wanted them to dream with me.

And they did. From that night on, they came up with some of the best ideas for a church launch I've ever heard, and now the Dream Team is what we call every person who serves in our church as a volunteer. Every year at the Dream Team party (where we thank people and celebrate with them) I remind everyone that it's not just gold-medal-winning Olympic athletes who are the ultimate team. It's people like them—and people just like you.

As we discussed in the chapter about the fourth cup, we experience ultimate fulfillment when we live out of our God-given purpose as part of a team. God said, "I will take you to be my people," not "my person." Of course, each person is God's child, his son or daughter; but in his promise to us, it's clear that we were created for a purpose that's bigger than ourselves. We were designed to be part of a cause, a movement, a mission. Without a doubt, this is what the body of Christ, the church, is intended to be.

God said, "I will claim you as my own people," and he honors his promise by making us part of his family, part of a team committed to making the only difference that really matters. You'll recall that the fourth cup is called hallel, or the Cup of Praise. When we drink from this cup, it's like trying to drink from a glass that's too full. When we raise it to our lips, it naturally overflows.

Experiencing the fourth cup is the ultimate sign of the mature work of God in our lives. Instead of feeling burdened by ministry, it feels like real joy, a selfless giving of who we are and what we're about. We feel connected to others and aware of the privilege of sharing our lives with theirs. If purpose is the real secret to happiness, then there's no happier person than the one who's making a difference.

Paul knew this secret—though he certainly didn't mind sharing it with everyone around him. He writes, "We do not lose heart. Though outwardly we are wasting away, yet inwardly we are being renewed day by day. For our light and momentary troubles are achieving for us an eternal glory that far outweighs them all. So we fix our eyes not on what is seen, but on what is unseen. For what is seen is temporary, but what is unseen is eternal" (2 Corinthians 4:16-18, NIV). Paul experienced trouble everywhere he went—storms, persecution, imprisonment, beatings—but he knew an abiding joy that never changed.

At our church, it's not about getting more volunteers to do more activities or complete more tasks. It's about people achieving a glory that outweighs the cares of life. It's about doing something eternal. To keep us focused on living out of the Cup of Fulfillment, we regularly ask ourselves, "Are people living fulfilled lives as part of a team that's making a difference?" Remember, success is when people are moving from where they are to where God wants them to be.

If you want your church to be planted in the living center of God's four cups of promise, then organize your ministry around *moving* people. I tell the folks at our church, "Move—or help us move people." It's the greatest adventure we can ever hope to experience, together with the most amazing people we can ever hope to know.

Some people say that today's church isn't relevant anymore, that it's old-fashioned and myopic and close-minded. If you know churches like that, it's a shame. Because that's not the living, Spirit-breathed, God-inspired, Christ-led kind of church that God has in mind. He calls us to live out of his four cups of promise.

We are his people and he has rescued us from slavery. Having freed us at last from the bondage of sin, he has now also delivered us from sin's power as we grow and mature. As if these two gifts aren't enough, God also redeems us—remember those Green Stamps?—and transforms our lives into his masterpiece. Finally, he allows us to be part of a family, a Dream Team of other brothers and sisters, committed to knowing and serving God because we love him so much.

In the traditional Jewish celebration of Passover, after the fourth cup, hallel, the participants recite a prayer that looks to the future and expounds on God's mercy and kindness. In the same spirit of joy, I offer this prayer to you:

> *May the God who parted the Red Sea for the Israelites as they fled Egypt part any obstacles in your life that would hinder your freedom. May you taste the exhilaration of not only your salvation, but also your deliverance from besetting sin. May you drink in the pursuit of your deepest dreams as your Father redeems your life and reveals your purpose. And may you savor the overflowing fulfillment of belonging to his family, forever and ever. Amen.*

NOTES

1. *State of Recidivism: The Revolving Door of America's Prisons*, The Pew Center on the States Public Safety Performance Project, April 2011, 2.
2. Rick Warren, "You Are Shaped for Significance" sermon series, © 2013 Saddleback Resources; http://www.saddlebackresources .com/006200_You-Are-Shaped-For-Significance-C944.aspx.
3. Tommy Barnett, interview at the Hillsong Conference, Sydney, Australia, July 3, 2013. The author was in attendance at this conference.
4. These descriptions of the expanded hierarchy of needs are adapted from Saul McLeod, "Maslow's Hierarchy of Needs," *SimplyPsychology*, published 2007, updated 2013; http://www .simplypsychology.org/maslow.html.

ACKNOWLEDGMENTS

To all my friends who offered support, encouragement, and assistance on this project, I am more grateful than you'll ever know. I'm especially indebted to

My wife, Tammy: You have been so loving and supportive in everything I have ever done. You are a gift from God and I will love you always.

My children, Sarah, Michael, David, Jonathan, and Joseph: Even though it takes so much time to do projects like this one, you always encourage me to do them. You understand what our lives are all about. I love you with all of my heart.

My assistant (and sister) Karol Hobbs: I simply couldn't do what I do without your help. Thank you for your hard work and devotion.

The Highlands Lead Team: Ronnie Bennett, Steve Blair, Hamp Greene, Denny Hodges, Scott Montgomery, Mark Pettus, and Layne Schranz: Through your faithfulness to God and these principles, a culture of intentional discipleship has been created at Church of the Highlands that has touched the lives of thousands of people. I love serving on the team with you.

My pastor, Larry Stockstill: Your love for God and passion for souls has inspired me for more than thirty-five years. Thank you for being a spiritual father to me.

My writer, Dudley Delffs: Thank you for working with me through this project and helping me clearly express these truths.

The whole team at Tyndale Momentum: Thank you for your commitment to spread the Good News of Christ around the world. I am so grateful for your friendship and partnership.

Jesus my King, most of all: Thank you for considering me faithful when I was faithless, and letting me play a small part in Your grand design. It is a joy to know You and serve You.

ABOUT THE AUTHOR

CHRIS HODGES is the *New York Times* bestselling author of *Fresh Air* and founding and senior pastor of Church of the Highlands, with campuses all across the state of Alabama. Since it began in 2001, Church of the Highlands has experienced tremendous growth and is known for its life-giving culture and focus on leading people to an intimate relationship with God. Chris is cofounder of the Association of Related Churches (ARC), which has launched hundreds of churches across America, and founder of the GROW coaching network. He is also founder and president of Highlands College, a ministry training school. Chris and his wife, Tammy, have five children and live in Birmingham, Alabama.

arc

association of related churches

Launching and growing life-giving churches

Are you a church planter or church leader, or do you belong to a church in transition? The Association of Related Churches (ARC) offers support, guidance, and resources in four key ways:

- *We help you start strong.* We show you how to build your launch team, raise funds, form a worship team, develop your children's ministry, and gain momentum—so you can open your doors with excellence. If you start strong, you have a greater chance of growing strong.

- *We reach the unchurched.* With more than 110 million Americans never or rarely attending church, it's critical that we cross cultural walls to reach the lost. ARC is all about helping churches stay culturally relevant—characterized by Bible-based teaching, authentic relationships, and dynamic family ministries.

- *We build relationships.* Solid relationships are the foundation for growth in any aspect of life. As ARC churches multiply across the country, you'll join an ever-expanding group of people who are committed to one another's success.

- *We support financially.* We know that it takes money to do ministry. That's why ARC invests financially into the vision of starting new churches.

For more information, visit ARC online at www.weplantlife.com.